Kingston Truman

A Step By Step Guide to Becoming A Millionaire

ISBN 978-952-93-5296-8

A STEP BY STEP GUIDE TO BECOMING A MILLIONAIRE

To the reader

I've tried many different paths to become rich. I also failed many times at it. Finally, I noticed that by developing certain characteristics it was actually possible for me to become a millionaire. This is a simple book with no jargon or otherwise difficult vocabulary. I made this book comprehensible so that anyone who is capable of reading, could learn without experiencing difficulties.

This book suits everyone, regardless of their age, gender or social status. Regardless if you are a student, a parent, a senior, a veteran, a well established businessman or uneducated trailblazer, this book will teach you how to make millions of dollars. The book carries a profound message backed up by real life experiences, different cases, deep knowledge and personal visions.

Sincerely

Kingston Truman

Table of Contents

CHAPTER 1 1

Building The Mindset Of A Millionaire 1

- Take control of your life 2
- You don't have to be special to become rich 4
- Climb from the bottom to the top 6
- Empty your mind 8
- Open your mind 11
- Change your way of thinking 13
- You get what you settle for 15
- Face the facts 17
- Develop thick skin 19
- Grasp the essentials of the "Can Do" – attitude 21
- Know when to take a timeout 23
- Get hungry and thirsty for success 25
- Understand That Your Possibilities Are Limitless 28
- Harness your inspiration 31
- Start thinking positive 34
- Organize your world 36
- Rock & Roll 38

Become self-disciplined 40
Start Controlling Your Mood 42
Understand the key factors that make success seeking people unsuccessful 45
Get rid of your fears 48
Stay in a good shape 50
Focus 52
Be passionate about what you do 54
The ABC of a Visionary 56
Have the right kind of modesty 58
Learn to understand how other people think 60
Keep reinventing yourself 63
Commit fully to what you do 66
Understand the idea of constantly making profit 67
Believe in yourself 69
Learn from yesterday– Focus on today – Build for tomorrow 71
Move out of your comfort zone 73
Understand the concept of money 75
CHAPTER 2 77
Practical principles 77
Build a strategy 78
Seize the opportunities 79

Be proactive 81
Keep it simple 83
Find your perfect Niche 85
Spot the demand and establish supply 87
Think globally 89
Generate wealth from your values 92
Fame equals money 94
Learn to productise anything 97
Turn your failures into success 99
Learn to work under pressure 101
Avoid taking debt 103
Be patient 105
Copy the successful people 107
Evolve on a daily basis 110
Work less, but be make more money – the profitable type of downshifting 113
The quickest path to riches is mostly full of risks and pressure . 115
Cut down your spending 117
Surround yourself by the right people 118
Be original 121
Always have a backup plan 123
Exceed everyone's expectations 124

Keep Track of Your Expenses and Profit.....125
Dress for success.....127
Learn New Skills.....129
Don't focus on getting million dollars, but rather on serving million people.....131
Share your burden by hiring professionals.....133
Time distribution and timing.....135
Develop customer oriented approach.....137
Beat your competitors.....139
Scale up your success.....141
Ensure your legal protection: patents, copyrights and agreements.....143
Make use of your true talent.....145
Become a great negotiator.....147
Learn to sell anything.....149
CHAPTER 3.....151
A Few Concrete Ways Of Making Millions.....151
Multitasking 101.....152
Marry a multimillionaire.....154
Get lucky at a game of chance.....156
Become a professional gambler.....158
Become a sports professional.....161
Hunt for the hidden riches.....163

Write and publish a book 166

Become a Hollywood actor 168

Make fortune in the real estate market 170

Invent something new 172

Use social media to get rich 174

Become an affiliate marketing wiz 176

Develop your career - work for a high salary 179

Become a public speaker 181

Epilogue 184

CHAPTER 1

Building The Mindset Of A Millionaire

Here's the truth: The millionaires think differently and unlike the vast population of low or average income.

So I'm going to tune you into the mindset of the millionaire.

Follow my advices and apply the lessons in your life!

Take control of your life

You need to stop being dependant on someone else's opinions. Your life is yours, period. What you do with your time, devotion and money should be ultimately up to you. Taking control requires responsibility and being strong enough to carry your own decisions with their consequences on your shoulders. You don't need to be extremely tough person to do that, but you can grow into the responsibility and begin taking control of your life by determining right now what you want in life and how you want to achieve it.

Actually, you could write down your plans and options on a piece of paper. Write how much money you want to make and also write all the possible ways of how you could make that money. This is an old trick, but it still works!

Don't victimize yourself

Have you ever complained to yourself or the others that you are a victim in your current situation? If you have done so, you probably have done it not once, but multiple times. Don't victimize yourself, but take control of your situation instead. By taking control of your life you create your own path, your own destiny and you certainly will have plenty of opportunities to become rich, but that requires you to step aside of your safe harbour and advance to the windy sea to catch bigger fishes that will bring you more money..

Are you miserable at the moment? If you are, then are you blaming someone else for it? Well, you shouldn't because the only one you can blame for your current situation is you! No matter who you are and what your situation is, you can always change for the better. Even if you were sitting in a prison cell, you can still become a better person a rich person because richness doesn't start with accumulating the money. Richness starts with developing a right kind of mind.

Stop making excuses

You might be saying that: "Well, I don't have the time", or "I'm not qualified enough". These are examples of excuses. In your life, you either *achieve results* or *make excuses.* You know what? Why don't you stop making excuses and start walking the walk because that's what's it going to take if you really want to achieve major success. You could be a one man army who has control of his inner battalion and achieve what thousands of demoralized trained soldiers can't achieve.

As an individual, you mostly have a poor judgement of knowing what's going on in our lives at the moment, especially if you are obsessed with some addictions that have the power of taking you down to the intellectual level of a caveman or erode you in any other ways.

A human being is capable of incredible things, but in order to achieve something he must first feel that he is in control of his decisions. That he is in control of his life. That is how we begin our journey, my friends.

You don't have to be special to become rich

When you walk on the street, sometimes you see people driving luxurious cars or performing on the stage in front of huge crowds, you think to yourself: "Wow! This person must be really special". You might not recall thinking like that, but often still feel that way in your subconscious. And why is that? Its embedded there by your parents and neighbours.

You might have been raised in a poor or middleclass home and had parents who have told them that: "Money doesn't grow on trees" or "Money is the root of all evil". Now that this sort of information has been programmed into your brain, it's no wonder why you see the rich as different species, different from the "average" folks.

But I'm here to declare you something: You don't have to be special to be rich. You don't have to be born under the lucky star to be rich. You don't have to have rich parents to be rich. You don't have to be super smart to be rich. The list goes on and on, but do you see my point here? You want to be rich. Let me tell you one thing. Richness is achievable. You can become a millionaire. You made a choice to begin your journey towards becoming one and you will not regret it, I personally guarantee you this.

No school will teach you how to be rich

There are simply no academic merits that can make you wealthy. All they can give you is some knowledge and academic accreditation, which applies for certain type of jobs when you are writing your applications to become hired. That's why you need to take lessons in another type of school. It's called the school of life. Most of the days you get an opportunity to learn several things whether you want it or not. You should definitely take advantage of those opportunities and learn from them as much as possible.

As humans we have the opportunity to develop ourselves in many levels. Even if you don't have the talent or special skills required to do something, it is highly likely that you reach your goal if you want it badly enough. Just keep practicing and keep trying and never give up!

The process of becoming rich

Many people like to romanticize even the process of becoming rich, but actually the process is not so romantic as we'd like to think. People, who earn their millions instead of winning or inheriting the money go through a process, during which they need to have their feet firmly on the ground while being focused on what they do. It's actually often very similar to everyday work, but it's just doing things on a much bigger scale.

You will need several different ingredients, which are mentioned in the following chapters of this book. By using these ingredients you can make your own private recipe which will make you a millionaire.

Climb from the bottom to the top

If you are starting from the bottom having very limited financial resources, getting rich might be a tough nut to crack. Actually it is not as tough as many think. The key here is to focus on *why you want to do* to get rich and *how can you accomplish it.*

Start climbing

The first question is why. Why do you want to become rich? To brag to your neighbours and friends? Or do you want to be rich so you could help your society? You are not the first one who have attempted to "climb the Mt. Millionaire". Only few have succeeded. Do you have the right motives that can take you to the summit? Some single mothers need to get two or three jobs just to be able to pay the bills. They have the right kind of spirit for the climbing task.

For most of us it takes years and years of practice through constant failures to achieve success. You know what Winston Churchill said?

"Success consists of going from failure to failure without loss of enthusiasm."

Write that down on several sticky notes and stick them everywhere around your house.

Obviously those who are afraid of failures aren't going to go far with achieving success. Now I want you to set some goals for yourself. Let's start from the base camp.

Setting goals

Start small. Set a goal for yourself; "I want to make that much money in total by the end of this year". There's also nothing wrong with thinking big, but it can be overwhelming at the beginning, so let start with something smaller. How would you like to be making twice the money you are making now by the end of this year?

It's possible. It's not impossible. Just put your head down, tune your brains for the challenge and start climbing from there.

Empty your mind

Do you ever feel that your life and especially your mind is filled with too many thoughts? When you make a decision that you want to turn your life around and become a millionaire, you need to let go of your old “me”.

Imagine that you are in the air on a hot air balloon. To reach the highest highs you need a lot of energy, but in addition to that you also need to let go of some of your ballasts that are keeping you down. Now picture dropping all those ballasts at once.

There’s a great technique for emptying your mind and it does not require any scientific technology or drinking alcohol. All you have to do is tell a lot of unnecessary secrets to the people who are close to you. This will clear some space in your mind, which is needed to craft your millions.

There is a state of mind called the *flow*. It was discovered by Mihaly Csikszentmihalyi. According to him flow is focused on motivation and harnessing emotions to improve your performance and learning. In my opinion emptying your mind from unnecessary stuff also helps you reach the state of flow. Now let’s have a quick peek at how draining your mind and self-inspiration can be reached metaphorically:

Once upon a time there was a guru who agreed to teach a young man how to become successful. He invited him on a beach at 4 AM and the young man came there dressed up in a suit. Now the guru told the young man to start walking into the sea. So he walked into the sea until the he was half submerged in the water. The guru told him to walk further away from the beach, so the young man walked there until the water reached his shoulders. The guru told him to keep walking. So he walked and eventually he was completely submerged. Then the guru held his head underwater until he almost passed out. Just before he passed out the guru pulled his head out of the water and told him: "You feel how much you wanted to breath? That's how much you need to crave for success!"

Escape from the prison of your own mind

Your mind can be your prison. There are plenty of negative thoughts that can lead to severely negative things even at physical level. Your own thoughts can also become your prison guards. They will control your life and make it miserable. You need to escape from this prison and never return to it again. That's just an example how your mind can potentially work. Being aware of this and not trusting your own thoughts too much can benefit you in the long run. You should be living this life through your instincts rather than though your thoughts and feelings. This way you increase your own performance and prevent the barriers of your mind to restrict your actions.

In order to feel good about building success, you need to reach a state of serenity. You can call it having "the good vibes" if you will, we need to be in harmony with the space surrounding us. We need to let go of all the negative stress signals and focus on performing and creating something in perfect serenity as well as we can. There are generally no known limits of how deep into this state you can go and for how long you can remain in this state. Sometimes it just activates all by itself and you can feel the good vibes paving the way for a great performance.

Open your mind

Now that your mind is opened, you can reach for the starts and get what you desire; in this case millions of dollars. Remember this mantra: "Life doesn't owe me a thing. I must forge my own success". Repeat this every morning, several times a day and before you go to sleep.

Fill your mind with the productive ideas which will benefit you in the long run. A lot of people think that they can get rich overnight. Don't focus on how to get rich instantly because it's requires luck, incredible talents and sometimes illegal actions. Focus how to create the persistent flow of income because that is what makes your efforts really worthwhile.

You have the keys to success, but you don't see them yet. You need to open your mind to discover the golden opportunities that slowly create the tiny streams of income that will slowly grow larger and possibly turn into passive streams of income. Picture that in your mind.

Now I want you to use your imagination. How do you think you would be able to create those streams?

There are great opportunities right around the corner just waiting to be discovered by you.

Over the time, people have found many new ways to get rich. A lot of old ways to get rich still work, but you need to understand something. Many young generations think nowadays that there's a secret fast-forward to the riches that doesn't require a lot of effort. This is utterly untrue. This is why once you set your mind to achieve the goal of getting rich, you will also need to be prepared to do a lot of work in order to achieve your success.

Opening your mind lets you see the productive ways to success in a wider perspective. It gives you a window to the field of big players, where you could make your big bucks. Just look at the biggest trailblazers of our time. Their mind was open and their imagination allowed them to visualize new possibilities to make money. In this context there are always two opposite ways of handling your mind. It's up to you, which one you will choose. Will you continue to dwell on the previous patterns of your mind or will you open your mind and let it lead you to success?

Change your way of thinking

If you keep on doing what you've always done ,you will keep on being what you've always been, nothing changes unless you make it change, I know what it sounds like, but every morning that I wake up I think about what that really means .Nothing Changes Unless You Make It Change.

Iris from the film: "The Samaritan"

I want you to stop and think of what will happen, if you do the same routines day by day while attempting to become rich without achieving great results? The chances are, you will fail. If you keep doing same things over and over again and expect different results from them, then you should get a date with a psychologist.

Some people will say: "Nobody ever changes". That's not true. Everyone can change if they work on themselves. And you don't need a university degree to become millionaire. Think of Bill Gates who dropped out of school and created Microsoft; one of the greatest companies of our time.

And let's face it: There is a high change of becoming rich as an entrepreneur. 4 in 5 billionaires made their millions by establishing their own companies. Registering a company is a relatively cheap investment, so go for it!

Too many people who never have worked as an entrepreneur, tend to think that even considering becoming one might be like a leap of faith, but you will never know how it will turn out for you if you never try becoming one. Once you want to become rich as an entrepreneur badly enough, you will start developing the mindset which will take you to the next level of thinking that you never thought existed!

You might be 25 years old and you read that someone 2 years younger than you just made a million dollars. How does that make you feel? Jealous? Make no mistake: Jealousy is actually one of the driving factors of many successful people. If you learn to channel it to give you strength and inspiration, jealousy will prove to be a useful asset to you. Harness the energy it gives to you and just do better than those you are jealous of.

You need rebuild your whole concept of thinking right now. Don't put it off for later, just seize the moment and start everything from a clean slate. Imagine that you are machine that produces money. You are a well engineered mechanical product that produces liquid cash and assets. Your task is to produce money for yourself. That's your top priority. I don't want to degrade your way of thinking to a primitive level, but frankly a goal oriented mindset pays off in the long run.

You get what you settle for

Our life always expresses the result of our dominant thoughts.

- *Soren Kierkegaard*

This is one of the things that many people don't understand. Our current situation in life reflects the result of our thoughts and actions. Or in other words you get what you settle for.

Sadly many of us settle for less than what they deserve. They set their own net worth threshold to whatever their earning a year and they get that just because they settle for it. Now imagine that you want luxury around you, nice cars and fabulous real estate. If you settle for achieving that you can actually achieve it, especially because so many other people have done it before you.

All you need to do is find a way how you can become a millionaire. I shall discuss a few different methods that help you accomplish that in detail later on, but before that you need to ask yourself: "Do I really want to be a millionaire?" If your answer is yes, then your one step closer to becoming unimaginably rich because really wanting it, is the first major step that needs to stretch all the way from beginning until the end of the process.

There is no limit to what you can achieve when you have a high goal ahead of you and you settle in for no less than that, but understand this: You mustn't settle for small things. You need to settle for big things. Now validate your cause. Ask yourself: "Why do I want to be a millionaire?". Search your feelings and be honest with yourself. If the answer is something like, I like "I don't really know why" or

"Everybody else is so rich" than there's really not a lot strength to your goal that you're settling in for, but if your answer is that: "I want to help my mother, who needs the money for a medical surgery", or "I need money for my kids, who are starving". I'm not saying that lack of what I call a proper motivation makes it impossible for you to become a millionaire. I state that it *validates* your cause. Each of us have their inner dialogues inside our minds. You can't really hear them or see them because their hidden from you. However, all the thoughts you have from waking up until going to sleep are part of your thought patterns, which you could actually alter cognitively.

You probably had those moments as a kid when you decided to do something. Something like biking all the way to grandma's house, even though it was tens of miles away in the rural area. It was tough and you thought you couldn't make it, but you settled for it with all your heart and mind and you achieve it because of that. That's why you really need to be completely convinced that becoming a millionaire is what you are settled for, but once you do settle for it, the rest will follow. Along the way you will grow stronger and smarter and will be able to make more decisions that will lead to prosperity.

Face the facts

Even though many of the famous frontrunners, innovators and other people who have made their success and fortune have often had their head in the clouds, they've mostly maintained their feet firmly on the ground. This is because they always need to be aware of the true status quo and what's really happening around them.

Sometimes you need to admit what's really going on, no matter how harsh the reality is. Pursuing something which was not meant for you for example is only going to waste your time and money. It requires some courage and modesty to admit that you failed for instance, but it's worth it because you can easily grow to your full potential out of moments like those.

You should never let your emotions or delusions deceive you. You need to learn how to return to the surface from the clouds.

Be brutally honest with yourself

I want you to be brutally honest with yourself. Every now and then you need to take look at the mirror and realize what you truly see there. Building a road to success in not a walk in the park. It's your personal journey where you really need to be yourself. Don't lie to yourself. Many who have done so, have gotten stomped one way or the other. You shape your world or your reality with what you do, but there is no room for staying at the back row of your life making excuses if you want to build your success. Excuses are for the losers. You live only once that's why it is time to take action and be the best you can be.

When you lie to yourself or knowingly pursue something that you know deep inside is not the right choice for you, you diminish the real you. If you've encountered a problem which you or anyone you know can't solve for you, face it and move on. If you have committed something immoral and you feel guilty, confess to yourself out loud that you have committed it. This will make you stronger and when you purify yourself like that, it's very likely that immediately you will feel tall as a mountain, strong as a lion and energetic like a bolt of lightning. You won't have the burden of self-deception on your shoulders and that will set your mind exclusively on what your true goal is.

Face your limits

You must also understand that even if you get a brilliant idea that you are not a superman. You can't do all the things by yourself in a short amount of time with minimum investments and maximum profit. As humans we tend to get fuelled by the impulses of passion. Sometimes we lack those impulses and at times like that, it's good to have a team that can create with you and inspire you. You should also face your mortality and the fact that your journey on this earth will end some day. The thought of that should encourage you to act while you still have the energy.

Nevertheless while you still continue your journey, there is no reason why you shouldn't give your 110% to achieve your goals. While our capabilities are limited, our imagination can be limitless. You should search for the breakeven point of your capabilities and imagination and act accordingly. That's how many great success stories are born.

Develop thick skin

Developing thick skin means that you shouldn't take criticism too personally. As you are building up your success, you must remain professional at many levels. There were, there are and there always will be those who will try to block your way, make things harder for you even just for the fun of it. Don't let them get under your skin.

There are many kinds of criticism that might irritate you. However, the constructive criticism is something you should take heed from. The negative criticism which undoubtedly tries to deprive you or your company of its value should be dealt with promptly. However, if the criticism is childish and harmless, then you should just let it bounce off of you. You got plenty of more important things to do than to react to the offenders who only by doing that are showing how low their morals are.

If you want to achieve success as a performer in show business, you need to be able to take the criticism and in some cases react to it publicly in the right manner. If you get seriously offended every time you get criticized, it's going to be emotionally tough for you to pursue your success altogether. The emotional burden of it might just get too tough for you at some point. Many who cannot handle negativity in publicly, often tend to seek comfort in vices such as drugs and alcohol. That's why the negative effect of being oversensitive to criticism usually accumulates and gets worse for you. So by staying tough you will also be able to maintain your mental health more easily and focus on building your revenue.

Now you know why it's important to develop thick skin and become immune to the criticism if it doesn't affect your public image. There are a few simple ways how you can build higher tolerance for the negative verbal arrows fired at you.

First of all, you need to embrace your working environment as your element, where you feel most productive. You need to maintain the ability to focus despite possible distractions. This you can achieve by neglecting all distractions by not assigning any value to them in your mind. You can simply just immerse yourself into the mood of productivity and what is necessary to grow your revenue. The "street critics" will not bother you much longer, if you ignore them completely. Another benefit of having thick skin is that you will be able to handle the problems that occur along the way. You will be stressing less when something doesn't go according to your plans.

Here's what the CEO and co-founder of Muse, Katheryn Minshew once said:

"Starting a business isn't for everyone and it's not what you should do if you aren't sure what else to do. It requires thick skin and the willingness to carry a great deal of stress, sometimes alone. It's more often a life of failure than a life of success and the majority of successes came after a long road of disappointment and often shame."

Grasp the essentials of the "Can Do" - attitude

Firstly, I'm going to tell you what a "Can Do" – attitude truly means and why it is so important to have it and lastly, I'm going to tell you how to find the right ingredients for it so you can develop your own Can Do – attitude.

Can Do – attitude is an attitude which amplifies your desire go get things done. It's a characteristic that describes mental strength. People with Can Do attitude will probably never say "I'm too tired", or "I can't do that". Instead, if they find out that they lack a skill that is necessary for accomplishing their task, they will do everything to learn it or get someone else to do it while supervising the completion of the task. Essentially a person, who is equipped with a Can Do – attitude lacks the capability to give up without doing their best. Do you recognize yourself as a person who gives up easily or who takes it to the limit? If you feel like you are a loser, it's time for a change. Tell yourself now that "I can do anything". It's time to become a winner.

Many people hope for a future where they don't have to run around all stressed up, struggling to pay the bills. By now you might have a hint of an idea that might make you a millionaire. There might also be some doubts in your mind, like "I don't have enough experience!" or "It's too difficult or time consuming for me!": By thinking like that, you are undermining yourself. You should be bigger than your problems! If you come up with a reason why you can't find a solution for a certain problem you are smaller than the problem. So all it takes is an attitude change, to overcome your problems. It takes a Can Do – attitude to build your own success. That's why people with Can Do – attitude become MILLIONAIRES.

The right amount of the Can Do – attitude

Can Do – attitude can be adapted in small portions or all at once. Whichever approach you take, it's for you to decide. Even if someone would ask you to build another Great Wall of China someplace else in the world, you will make it happen because you have a can do attitude. Can Do – attitude is basically channelling your thoughts and energy and focusing on whatever needs to be done and excluding the option of backing out of it.

A person with the Can Do – attitude will sooner or later come up with a solution, while someone else might cause more problems. After harnessing your attitude, you'll feel like you can do anything! And when you set your mind to do something there's a great chance you will be successful at it.

Move fearlessly toward your goals

So wrap yourself around the mentality of Can Do – attitude and move fearlessly towards your goals. The importance of actions can be shown in the following quote, spoken once by Winston Churchill:

"I never worry about action, but only inaction".

Know when to take a timeout

Even though as individuals we are capable of reaching unimaginable levels of productivity, it's always good to mind the fact that we are only humans. In order to avoid serious burnout we need to take a timeout every now and then. There are several things that enhance the possibility of emerging burnout, such as rapid build up of the pressure. If it gets too rough for you, it's ok to take a break from it all and clear the pressure for a while.

The best way to take the timeout is by changing the atmosphere for a while. Basically it means taking a vacation from work. The duration of your timeout depends on how much time you can afford to stay off work and how much time you need to be able to recover.

Sometimes even a small nap during the day is an effective way of taking timeout and relieving pressure. In fact, these days many notable organizations know this and have even set up special nap rooms for their employees to take occasional naps. By staying fresh you also increase your productivity level and that's a state that you often need to immerse yourself into if you want to make some serious money.

Even if you have a lot of responsibilities you shouldn't let those responsibilities take their toll on your health. So every day you should spend a few hours just relaxing . This decreases the amount of acids in your stomach. Your heart rate slows down and your system tones down, which prevents the risk of cardiac diseases.

Taking a timeout does not only help you reinvigorate you physically, but it also allows you to form another perspective to your problems, which might tremendously help you find effective solutions to them.

Continuing work for over 8 hours in a row without having any breaks not only affects your working capability, but it also tones down your ability to think creatively.

It would be great for you if you could structure your working rhythm in a way that it would include breaks or timeouts every now and then. There should be phases that would allow you to charge your batteries and then keep on going again. For the sake of productivity, the timeouts and the phases should be organized in a consecutive and seamless pattern.

Get hungry and thirsty for success

Success is not a dish that is served to you whenever you want it. It's something you really need to work for. It's something you need to put your sweat and blood into. It's a special treat meant for those who want to achieve something more than the average. So develop your hunger for success so that it comes in line with your natural instincts.

There are no general outlines of how to build your appetite for success because people tend to react differently to different things. For instance you could imagine yourself being poor for the rest of your life. That vision of you being old, poor and miserable sparks hunger for making money in some people. Others are more motivated by looking at successful people, their expensive cars and their fabulous lifestyle.
If you manage develop a sustainable hunger and thirst for success, it's going to be your top priority to do whatever is necessary to achieve it. Going a few extra miles while trying to turn your dream into reality will feel like a walk in the park.

There are various types of success that are available for you in forms of various dishes. You just need to put some effort to get to enjoy them. So many people before you have developed hunger and thirst for success and taken all the measures necessary to become wealthy and financially secured, so why wouldn't it be possible for you as well? You could be the next big thing in the Forbes magazine. You could be a billionaire, but it's not going to happen unless you really want it.

Life flows by whether you are doing something productive or not. What truly matters is what you can do with the time that is given you. It's the steps you make towards your final goal that count. Albert Einstein once said:

Outstanding personalities are created through hard work and its results.

He also said:

"If you want to live a happy life, tie it to a goal, not people or objects".

From these aphorisms we can derive that success requires A – hard work and B – goal oriented life that also results in a life full of happiness. Having an outstanding personality and reaching happiness can already be counted as success on smaller scales, but with regard to success that we are talking about; with regard to becoming a millionaire, these two things: outstanding personality and happiness, are actually your personal characteristics that help you achieve your material success.

There is no genie in the bottle that can fulfil all your wishes, but if there were, having found the magic lamp, would you ask the genie to make you rich? If so would you be able to enjoy your riches? Actually fortune gathered by "cheating" doesn't feel deserved. It's the basic human nature. It only builds up greed. So it's better to strive for not only the increase of capital on your bank account, but the increase of deals and victories that you achieve along your path.

If you are not sure whether you are hungry and thirsty enough, you can make a following test: Go to sleep, wake up. What will be the first dominant thought that comes on your mind? If it's something else than building your success, then you are definitely not hungry and thirsty enough. Keep testing yourself like this until one day you wake up and the first idea on your mind will relate to building up your success.

Understand That Your Possibilities Are Limitless

Hey, did you know that you can achieve anything in your life? There is no limit to what you can achieve if you are willing to take the necessary steps. "So what are the necessary steps?", you might ask. First and foremost you have to free yourself from the primitive structure of your mind. If you only dream about achieving success, but in the same time think that it's impossible for you to actually achieve, then you are a prisoner of your own mind. Sometimes you just need to remove all the artificial elements of your life, the elements that are restricting you to life up to your full potential.

You shouldn't underestimate yourself by imagining that you are inferior to all the famous and successful people. They didn't build anything perfect, they only made it seem as if it's perfect. It takes years of practise to achieve that on average. Some of us are naturally more talented than others at something and might have a strong business oriented mind, which allows to turn their talent into a profit magnet. That's why you should never think that it's too late for you to spread your wings and reach for the stars. Don't tell yourself that you are too old or undereducated or not intelligent enough. You just have to step into the unknown and do something new, something that you feel is close to your heart and something you would like to do for the rest of your life.

No matter which path you choose there are always opportunities and paths to success you can always embark on, so you shouldn't restrict your activities to some specific types of business. Surely the fields you are most interested in and most educated at would be your best bet, but many millionaires have been successful at several different business fronts. By diversifying your ventures, you also bring more sustainability to your profit pattern. The keyword is persistence. Depending on how persistent you are, you can achieve unbelievable results even with limited proficiency. You do not need to be an Einstein to become a millionaire.

If you are applying for jobs or you are looking for clients, selling your product, you can always be more efficient. You can do more in less time. You can also do the same with better quality. Think about what and how you should improve. You might think that you are bad at what you do or dwell on similar depressive thoughts. You're not the only one. That shouldn't stop you from trying to reach something greater than you.

There's a brilliant quote by Ralph Marston that says:

"You've done it before and you can do it now. See the positive possibilities. Redirect the substantial energy of your frustration and turn it into positive, effective, unstoppable determination."

And here's what Stephen Hawking says about possibilities in the context of past and future:

"The past, like the future, is indefinite and exists only as a spectrum of possibilities."

Harness your inspiration

When you're truly inspired, you need to get the most out of it. There are moments in your life when you get seriously inspired and that non-stop inspirational moment might last from few seconds to several days. Whichever way you are using to become a millionaire, you must learn how to harness your inspiration as much as possible.

Sources of inspiration

So where can you get the inspiration? There are plenty of motivational videos on YouTube for example. Just choose your topic and you will see the results. In our case, we want to become rich. Just use the relevant keywords, like "rich, motivational speech" and you will be sure to find some inspirational clips of speakers who fill you with inspiration.

After you've received your dose of inspiration, don't waste time! Start planning immediately on how to build up your success. We tend to distract ourselves with awful lot of unnecessary things that kill our inspiration and lull us into the mood of ignorance. Our inspiration on the other hand, if mixed with imagination, is like a huge garden or an endlessly spacious department store with limitless variety. You can pick whatever you like and apply it to what you're doing. Many of the modern song writers have been inspired by the musical productions of older generations and so it was before them. If you are creating something that requires originality however, you should always check if someone has already created an innovation just like yours before you.

Turning inspiration into tangible matter

If you learn how to put your inspiration into tangible matter like words for example, you could be looking at great moneymaking opportunities. There's no better feeling than the one you get from creating something out of thin air and turning it into profit. Right now, thousands if not millions of people are looking for someone to create them something for big money. If you are certain of the continuation of your inspiration, why not become an entrepreneur and set your own prices? If you do everything properly, you will be having loads of clients who rush to purchase a piece of your production, which is the courtesy of your talent mixed smoothly with your inspiration.

Some achievements require the efforts of a group of people that is equally inspired. The wisdom can be found in the words of Queen Elisabeth the II:

"I know of no single formula for success, but over the years I have observed that some attributes of leadership are universal and are often about finding ways of encouraging people to combine their efforts, their talents, their insights, their enthusiasm and their inspiration to work together."

It's obvious that you need to harness your inspiration while you have it in you, so make sure that you use all the inspiration you get as effectively as you can.

Start thinking positive

Thinking positive can actually make you rich among other things of course. The ability to think positive even in situations which seem hopeless have often lead to breakthroughs, turnaround and unimaginable success stories.

It does not take a lot of effort to start thinking positive. The common misconception about the positive thinking is that people who only think positive are often considered weird. In some cultures positive thinking is part of the local ways. The truth is people who think positive often have a high work ethic, which makes them work diligently to achieve their goals.

Positive thinking can actually give you that extra boost of confidence you need to create something. It can overshadow the negative things and help you stay focused on what's important. By staying positive you reduce your stress level even when different things like deadlines or problems build up the pressure.

If you achieve success through thinking positive, you will not spin out of control as a result of your success. That's because you knew you were going to become successful before actually achieving your goal. And even if things don't go your way, by staying positive you minimize the recoil of the possible setbacks you will endure along the way.

Optimist vs. pessimist

Optimist sees opportunity in every challenge, while the pessimist sees challenge in every opportunity. Those who are keen on hunting opportunities, are opportunists. Opportunists have a lot of positive qualities in themselves because those qualities result in mental requirements necessary to overcome the tough obstacles. On average, an optimist can handle a setback more cheerfully than a pessimist, but on the other hand the pessimist always expects a setback and he is capable of predicting them more accurately than an optimist.

So your best bet would be combining the best qualities of optimism and pessimism. The combination that will be formed out of that equation will give you a great head-start in your pursuit of riches. You can't trust your judgement as a meter for your development process in this field, but the results will speak for themselves. The way you will tackle the difficulties and obtain new deals will show the new side of you that you may have never seen before.

Here's Harvey Macay's intake on positive thinking:

"Positive thinking is more than just a tagline. It changes the way we behave. And I firmly believe that when I am positive, it not only makes me better, but it also makes those around me better."

Now that you have read this chapter, you probably have already begun to understand how positive thinking truly shapes your world.

Organize your world

When I'm talking about your world, I'm talking about everything that you have control over. That means your apartment or house, workplace or the desktop of your computer. By staying organized your mind will correlate with it and you will start thinking more clearly. If your apartment is a mess then clean it first. You will also need to clean your computer desktop. That will help you to become more organized.

Clarity of mind is needed for important decisions and you will be making a lot of important decisions along the way of becoming a millionaire. Of course you can't keep all the things in order 24/7, but you can certainly try to fix your current state of mind by getting things in order. Chaos can be created momentarily and it often seems as if it is being formed all by itself. Organizing, on the other hand, takes hard work and dedication.

Reorganizing your state of mind

Everybody has bad days. Every now and then things don't go your way and you will feel down and depressed. Your apartment might be a mess and the condition of your relationships might not be at its best. That's why it's important to do a grand clean up. This can be done by cleaning everything, setting all your relationships in order, wearing newly washed clothes, getting all the karma debt off your shoulder basically reboots your state of mind. You will feel clean and fresh.

As soon as you set your newly organized life for success, start maintaining the organization of things around you. We all know how easy making a mess is and how hard it can be to clean up. Organize your surroundings and keep it as your routine. Your newly created order will reflect on many different levels.

Organize your thoughts

Having unnecessary secrets in life and being too dependent on other people can become a real burden for you. Unnecessary secrets are like dams in your mind, the pressure is corroding your life. When it comes to being dependent on other people, I suggest that you should always think at least a few steps ahead and organize your future by maintaining a high level of self-sufficiency. By being as self-sufficient as you can, you reward yourself with peace of mind and better quality of sleep.

Ursus Wehrli once said:

"One way to organize your thoughts is to tidy up, even if it's in places where it makes no sense at all."

When you think of it, it actually makes sense. Even if you don't notice the disorder around us, in your house or workplace, we still lack a sense of tidiness in our heads. Even if just the idea of cleaning up sounds like too much of work, the result it gives is worth the effort many times over.

Rock & Roll

"Wait... did I just read Rock & Roll?", you must be thinking. Yes you did, but I'm not going to tell you about the music itself. In this context, Rock & Roll is a metaphor of "going wild and crazy". You will need Rock & Roll to let it go, to relax and chill, get wild, get crazy, smile and laugh. Were not at a graveyard tour here. Sometimes you just need to go with the wind, hop on a plane and do what you want for a while.

Do you know a song that fills you with energy and makes you feel great? Turn it on and let it work its magic on you. You should, however, know the limits of your Rock & Roll. Don't let it become a negative aspect of your life. Use it as an energizing tool to inspire you and boost your creativity.

Get empowered by music

Each morning, when you start your daily success building routines, I personally recommend to turn on a special song, something that gives you "the good vibes" and conditions your mind for achieving success of no less than epic heights. It energizes you to get down to business, to stop speculating and start taking action. That's why many professional athletes listen to this kind of music before they begin performing at competitions. The music can be key factor that sets your mind for an explosive performance.

If music helps you focus then it's definitely a good idea to keep your favourite radio channel or your favourite band or song playing while you are doing something highly valuable. If the music is not fit for the surrounding environment or inappropriate for the people who surround you, you can always be listening to it through a portable music device like a MP3 – player for instance.

It's been stated that some types of music like classical music actually improve your concentration and overall performance of your brain. However, you shouldn't just leave it at that. Keep your intellectual skills sharp for new challenges.

Surroundings don't matter – objectives do

Building success doesn't need to appear as some sort of struggle, but it can be fun and you can decide which spice you want to add to it. You are the creative genius and you can keep your painter's workshop as messy as you want, but to justify it, let's say only if you are on your way to becoming the next Picasso for example. As long as you think objectively, you don't care what surrounds you. What matters is the final goal and what it takes to reach it.

Never underestimate the efforts required to reach your objective. Often you need to be fully in sync with what you do to produce better output. Or sometimes you just need to give it a 100%. Nothing good comes out of mediocre efforts and slacking. Let your inner music or the outer tunes guide you to your dreams. Let it inspire you to create something unforgettable. Let it pave the way for your success.

Become self-disciplined

Millionaires and billionaires have often been asked: "What's the key to success?" The answers have varied case by case, but one keyword has emerged out of the pool of answers: Discipline. Discipline, especially in a form of self-discipline, is something that has turned dwarves into giants. It is a virtue that is beyond many other virtues in the context of success.

Discipline is basically a smooth mix of willpower and self-control. One of the best things about discipline is that your mind is able to turn it into one of your "primary settings", but that does never come by default. The discipline is something that can be only obtained by making your mind and body comply to harsh but in the same time beneficial standards. The standards won't result in sustainable income if you don't fully accept their necessity and affirm their beneficial impact on your life.

Once upon a time, many centuries ago, there was a Greek city It's citizens and especially warriors were known for their exceptional discipline. The warriors of that city had exceptional success on the battlefields and known for their fearless, furious and relentless performance. They went from victory to victory. Those warriors were called Spartans. You probably have heard how only 300 Spartans held back an enormous army of Persian soldiers. The Spartans were heavily outnumbered and they still held their ground valiantly.

You can become disciplined by prioritizing the things that are most beneficial to your:

- health
- habitat
- business
- social life
- prosperity

As if following the discipline driven success of the Spartans many successful individuals that got their names in the books of history have lived by the same rules. Being disciplined might be harsh, but it doesn't mean that you will stop enjoying your life. On the other hand if you are 100% confident that you can reach success without being disciplined, just go for it. Life full of discipline only facilitates reaching your goals, but it's not an obligatory requirement for reaching those goals.

You can never expect your business partners to be disciplined, but you can always inspire them if you are highly disciplined yourself. When you choose your partners, you can notice their level of discipline. For example, if they maintain a good level of communication and move forward with your mutual projects without unexplained delays, you can say without a doubt that they are disciplined. If your success depends on your partners even to the lowest extent, you must ensure that your partner can maintain a proper level of discipline and responsibility in order to get things done. Otherwise you might be risking time and money.

Start Controlling Your Mood

Never underestimate the ability to change your mood in a split second. Sometimes you need to be a social chameleon that blends in effectively. At social events, your mood is your camouflage that helps you building your network, even though deep inside you might be feeling bad due to some personal issues. You can become a successful influencer by transforming from a conservative spectator into a charismatic speaker.

Controlling your mood means switching cognitively from one mood to another. Every time you wake up you automatically have a physical stress condition on. You might not notice it, but your brain is consuming a lot of serotonin, which is common in stressful situations. You probably feel tired, hungry or pissed off. I call it the auto mood – which is your default mood, triggered by your condition or the surrounding environment.

Overriding the auto mood

Your auto mood can be overridden by few easy steps. Firstly, you need psyche yourself. Secondly, you need to harness all your attention and energy to the project at hand. All the anger, frustration and aggression can be channelled to produce something valuable. You needn't be the prisoner of your mood. You can learn to control it by kicking in the right mood gear, when its necessary. You need to understand that your own mood *can* be controlled and by influencing your own mood you can also influence the mood of those around you.

Significance of the mood alteration

In order for your mood alteration to be more effective, you need to fully understand the significance of it. Obviously changing mood cognitively is important because you require it to achieve progress in some particular situations. It can be an asset to you, whether you are alone or surrounded by other people. When you are alone, your mood alteration can lead to better concentration and it can also intensify your efforts thus bringing you better results.

It's extremely easy for anyone to just lay back start watching TV, drinking beer. While most see this as a relaxation method, it actually degrades you and often makes it more difficult for you to switch your productive mood back on. That's why reading books and doing sports during your free time is much more effective method of improving the continuity of your progressive mood.

Autosuggestion really works

Autosuggestion is basically suggesting yourself or hypnotizing yourself to believe something. For instance if you are at your most productive mood at mornings, you could autosuggest in the afternoon that it's morning. Do a few morning chores and the morning mood will kick in fresh. You can repeat this several times a day and you will be packed with productive energy all day long.

As soon as you learn to take your mood under control, you will start noticing significant changes in your life. You will feel better and you will be more active, but most importantly of all in this case: You will have mastered one of the characteristics of a future millionaire. The mood you achieve now, is the mood that will potentially take you a long way and help you get the things done that are required to become mega rich. If you are digging gold and having lazy moods popping out all of a sudden, how do you plan on ever hitting that gold vein? So stay in control of your mood and keep up the good work.

Understand the key factors that make success seeking people unsuccessful

The amount of millionaires compared to the global population is very low. If dollars would grow on trees, we would be all rich, but there are certain key reasons why some of those who have pursued success haven't actually achieved it.

First and foremost, they aren't doing the right things and some of them are, they aren't spending enough time doing that and because of their lack of "millionaire qualities", they will keep spending too much time, without gaining proper results. Some of the success driven cases that have ended up unsuccessful are just bouncing around without having a clear direction. They often think that they can do everything by themselves and often end up having a burnout.

Another reason why some people are unsuccessful is because they simply don't want to step out of their comfort zone. They don't want to even imagine taking risks. They mostly just follow their own perceptions of how everything works and end up empty handed.

The struggle

There are plenty of other reasons involved, but if success is one of the things you truly want to achieve in your life and despite of struggling to achieve it for many years you haven't managed to achieve it, you should really walk up to the mirror and ask the person you see in front of you: "Why aren't you successful?". This is basically stepping out of yourself and judging yourself neutrally from a third person perspective. You need to establish the key ingredient of your failures in order to fix your approach to success. If it's too troublesome for you to find out, you should consult with those who have been in similar situations and managed to turn the situation around in their favour. Building a road to riches isn't commonly as romantic or beautiful as you might have thought it would be. It's utterly robust, that's all I can say out of my experience. It takes hard work. You need to get your hands dirty and start sweating to approach the true success inch by inch. Imagine you are digging a well under a burning sun. At first it seems rough and unforgiving or even seemingly pointless, but as you dig deeper into the ground you start noticing hints of water and digging gets easier as your motivation rises with the sight of the ground water filling the bottom of the well. The tougher your efforts, the sweeter the prize.

Helping others

According to some, many people who strive for success but remain unsuccessful, can be even considered egocentric. The formula works like this: You're supposed to help others and get paid for it. Here's a quote from a world famous speaker Brian Tracy:

"Successful people are always looking for opportunities to help others. Unsuccessful people are always asking, 'What's in it for me?"

Haven't you wondered why so many successful millionaires start doing charity work? It's because they want to keep helping people, but this the formula is upside down: They are paying to help others.

Get rid of your fears

Many of us have some kind of fears. Some say that fears are part of our self defence mechanism, embedded in our DNA to keep us safe. Fears can also be reminders of our traumatic experiences.

Face your fears

Facing ones fears might sound like a clique, but it's actually a very wise advice. You need to take a closer look at your fear without any prejudice and start examining them or running some tests on them, like a scientist. This way you your fear becomes less threatening because you're starting to understand what you're dealing with.

I'm going to be very clear with you, it takes guts and self determination to become rich if you start poor. If you have fears like social anxiety, how can you expect to get paid big for something that requires at least some form of social interaction?

Also, you can't let uncertainty control you. Uncertainty can easily occur for you in a situation, where you are afraid to make a decision. You should understand that when things are going well for you, you shouldn't be afraid to raise the bets and to scale things up to make more money.

Case of A Historical Conqueror

No matter what the object of your fear is, it will always create a barrier between you and success. You should be fearless like the historical figures who built their empires hundreds of years ago. I'm talking about Alexander the Great, I'm talking about Gengis Khan and many others. The essential step for them to become rules of a gigantic empire was to fight wars and conquer nations. They showed example to their troops by facing the enemy on the battlefield in the frontlines. What would have happened, if they were afraid of fighting? What if even the thought of a battle would have given them shivers? Should that be the case, they probably wouldn't have become historically famous. You shouldn't let your fears become determining factors of your failure.

Here's what Charles Stanley stated about fear:

"Fear stifles our thinking and actions. It creates indecisiveness that results in stagnation. I have known talented people who procrastinate indefinitely rather than risk failure. Lost opportunities cause erosion of confidence and the downward spiral begins."

So are you still thinking of remaining seated comfortable on your couch and drawing the imaginary monsters in the back of your head or will you take action and go full steam towards success? It's up to you to decide.

Stay in a good shape

Mens sana in corpora sano (A sound mind in a sound body)

- *Juvenal, a Roman poet*

Even the ancient Romans knew about the interconnection between mind and body. They knew that preserving your health also preserves your mind. So make sure you take a good care of your health. There are many effective forms of exercise that help you shape your mind in the right direction. Speaking of which, there's one form of exercise that's designed especially for the mind. It's called meditation. By meditating effectively you will also be more effective in finding the right solutions to your problems and creating new ways of making loads of money.

By being physically fit, you have the energy for your inner machine to create things and make them happen. You don't need to be as fit as a professional athlete, but you need to be strong to be on top of things and to be able to endure the setbacks. If you don't take care of your health and constant pressure keeps you on the edge of getting sick, how can you be able to carry on walking on the road to riches?

So remember this:

1. Always take care of your physical health
2. Never do anything which would harm your health substantially
3. Don't put your life at risk

As mentioned above, it's important to take care of your health by keeping your body in good shape. It's also worth saying that excessive smoking does not take you closer to millions of dollars. It only wastes your money and health. Putting your life at risk would also be a foolish thing to do and you should think of the ways to preserve your health in order to stay fit and capable of making money in the long run.

The importance of a good night's sleep

Sleeping is much more important than many of us think. The quality sleep has a wide range of health benefits. You could even lose weight more easily by sleeping well, but most importantly sleep is essential for our brains to function optimally. That's why you should always try to get your 6-8 hours of sleep per night. Skip sleeping only on extreme circumstances, unless you can go just fine without sleeping that much.

Focus

Have you ever been at musical concerts or perhaps a circus? If you have, then you probably have seen some great talents out there performing and using their magnificent skills. Their talents and skills might differ from one another, but there is still something that each and every one of them have also mastered. It's called focus.

The essence of focus

Focus is basically high level of attention that is essential to perform something which requires a great deal of concentration. For many of us it's very easy to lose focus. In fact, it might be as easy to lose it as it is difficult to gain it back. Some people boost their focusing skills by doing yoga or meditation. Whatever it is you're doing to improve your focusing abilities, you need to keep in mind that it's an essential ingredient of your success.

How to focus

The best way to focus is to leave everything else out of the equation like problems at home and problems at work. For example, someone close to you passed away, you got divorced, the bills keep piling up and so on. You will address those issues when the time is right, but when you really need to focus, you can't let any irrelevant thoughts disrupt your concentration. Have you ever had those days when you look at your wristwatch or the bigger clock on the wall and notice the time being 9 AM and after a while, which seemed like a moment later, you check the time again and notice that the time is already 4 PM? It's as if the time just flew by. Focusing leaves you also more content with your results. If you keep surfing online or chatting with your colleagues every now and then, you probably don't care about your job that much and chances are that you might get fired sooner or later.

Focusing on your work might be tough when you have a lot of freedom. Those who work from home can easily let their focus slip, which will lead to loss of time and probably even money.

How to maintain long term focus

Maintaining long term focus might sound like a difficult task, but it really isn't one. What you need is some other people working next to you or working on the same project in another location. You'll become more responsible, when there's other people who's success also depends on your contribution. That's why focusing is usually the biggest challenge for those who are self employed with continuous external income flowing into their accounts.

If your work is the only source of your income and you don't have a backup plan, then you are probably more eager to contribute and focus on it. If you experience a short term lack of focus, just watch a motivational speech on YouTube.

Be passionate about what you do

If you show a lot of effort in order to become rich but don't have the passion for what you are doing, then how do you expect to deliver the necessary results every day of the week, every week of the month for several years? I wouldn't have even considered writing this book, unless I was passionate about teaching people how to become rich. So let's talk about passion.

Essence of passion

Passion is the way you can be bound to different things, your job, your hobby or your loved ones. It's fundamentally a form of burning desire for something. You could say that it comes from your heart, but it also affects your state of mind. Passion can spice up your life, resulting both in positive and negative outcome. I'm going to teach you how to harness all the positive elements of passion and turn them into your driving force.

Even when you are physically and mentally tired, the passion can fuel you and keep you going like an energy drink. It is like a magic potion that makes you want something intensively and makes you do whatever it takes to achieve the necessary results. However, passion is not reached without certain measures.

Prioritize your moneymaking

Each activity that makes you money now or in the future needs to be set to a high priority level in your life, so that you could fuel yourself with that passion, but remember: Your passion must always be directed into providing you pure energy and creativity. If you set moneymaking as your top priority, then all you need to do is to use passion as your rocket fuel.

The right kind of passion

All of us are different and there's not a single formula for the right kind of passion. There are certain ways to know if you actually have the right kind of passion in yourself. It comes from the heart and it makes you feel great when your do what you are passionate about. However, if your passion is a fierce state of mind, where you don't actually enjoy what you are doing, then it's not the right kind of passion at all. It could turn into work craze or workaholism to be more exact.

When you let passion become your source of energy, you will create things that will flame your passion to burn brighter and that continues as a loop. It's like a perpetual cycle which will push you to success sometimes without you even noticing it.

Let's wrap up this topic with a quote from Oprah Winfrey:

"Passion is energy. Feel the power that comes from focusing on what excites you."

The ABC of a Visionary

Not everyone has got the ability to look into the future. I'm not talking about fortune tellers. I am talking about the people who can think ahead. They can look into the future by using their imagination or by creating projections of possible scenarios that are based on facts. If this sounds too complicated, I'm not going to antagonize you with difficult phrases any further. Let's have a look at an example.

There was a time when Donald Trump, a great American tycoon was just starting his own business. He saw an opportunity and gathered a lot of influential people around him and shared his vision with them. It was a risky game, he wasn't a millionaire when he started off, but because he was brave enough to fulfil his vision, he became one.

I'm going to tell you what it takes to achieve that mindset. Your dream is to become rich, am I right? Why don't you first vision yourself doing something which would get you tons of money? Now modify your dream to be as realistic as possible. Just envision yourself starting doing that thing which makes you tons of money. Now all you have to do, is to have the initiative to go out there and get it done! It's that simple. It's all about transforming your dreams into realistic and reasonable form. From there on out, your dream can become essential part of your everyday life.

When you visualize something that you want to accomplish, you need to be very specific. Unspecific visualizations often tend to result in failures. By specifying your dream, it's instantly becomes much more tangible and easier to follow.

Be the architect of your dreams by visualizing the outlines of your goals and then just take action. You might be nervous when stepping on this exciting path, but don't worry, you're not the first one to set your foot on it! Also, don't let the small mistakes here and there bring you down. Your vision is your roadmap to success. Follow it's blueprints and you will see that building success is much easier than you thought!

Have the right kind of modesty

Ages before Gengis Khan built his Asian empire, Attila The Hun was the fearless warlord who lead his troops to historical battles. When Attila received guests, he treated them to exotic foods which were put on golden and silver plates, while Attila himself only ate meat from a wooden plate. And when you think of it, characters like humility really seem to be the fundamental building blocks of a sustainable empire.

As the old saying states, the pride sooner or later leads to fall. Therefore you should harness modesty as a part of your mindset. You must realize that you are not perfect, but you can still achieve great success. Every day you can contribute to your master plan to a certain extent. Every day you can add some essential bits to it, but if you think that you are doing a great deed to the world when you're only contributing to your personal success then the process itself will suffer tremendously. On the other hand if you are working with a group of scientists on a scientific breakthrough, you can cognitively wrap your mind around of the significance of your work, but even then thinking about how important your work is will not enhance the quality of your success.

There are many superstars in Hollywood and music business who aren't arrogant and prudent and yet their success speaks for itself. Many of them are just working very hard. They can put their head down and really give their 110% in order to reach success. After all, we are all equal And you have an equal chance of making a difference in your personal life and in the life of other people. You can even change the world someday, but because the world isn't functioning in a way that grants you automated success, you really need to show substantial amount of work ethic to achieve great things in your life.

So as you can see, modesty will pave the way to a great work ethic, which drives you towards success. Keep following that path properly and you will reach your goal.

Learn to understand how other people think

Learning to understand the patterns of thoughts going through other peoples mind, is an important attribute to your skills, no matter what your trade is. Even if you were trading stocks in your room, wouldn't it be useful to know what goes through the minds of the hundreds if not millions of other traders as well? Because if they unilaterally decide to buy a certain stock en masse, then its price will spike quickly and by reading those patterns and essentially what goes through the mind of traders at moments like that can be a million dollar attribute to your trading portfolio.

If you are a retail store owner, wouldn't it be handy to imagine being a customer and looking at your store from customers perspective? Yes it would. You would spot the flaws more easily, making you more prone to improving the flaws more promptly. That's why it's useful to be able to get what the person in front of you is all about. If you are recruiting people in your dream team, you should be able to read the applicants while listening to the worlds they are telling you.

Everything around you and that you have control over can be divided into assets and liabilities. Even the employees. If we are talking about your employees, you need to understand the hidden motives behind the reason why a certain employee suddenly underperforms for example.

Knowing how other people think isn't that difficult as you might think. It requires analyzing the people around you. It's undoubtedly easier to know a lot about the people that you have known for years in comparison with total strangers. However, reading total strangers isn't impossible. The small hints allow us to read other people like a book. Those hints are usually details like: clothing, rings, posture, walking style, voice, gestures and so on. By paying more attention to deciphering the patterns of human behaviour you get deeper understanding of other people. You realize the logic behind their thinking and get access to new possibilities when interacting with those people.

You might have a modest start, but as you progress, you will learn how to find out all the essential things about another person within the matter of seconds. This comes in handy, especially when you are negotiating with people that you have never met before. In order to achieve the best results, you need to find the common ground with other people. The same strategy works for example in achieving a romantic date with someone you really like.

If you are building a dream team, afterunderstanding what someone else is really about, you should learn how to affect and inspire them. After adopting your dream , you'll get much closer to achieving your success. The more different people you get from different backgrounds and with different specializations to work for you in a likeminded passion, the better the results. Everyone will be fully dedicated and that's something you can truly enjoy and be proud of.

Depending on how you treat people you can either get a lot of friends or a lot of enemies. The outcome might be completely neutral as well, as you can stay more or less under the radar. When people open up to you, you better treat them well and with respect. They will be thankful to you and might reward you unbelievable opportunities. If you mistreat them, they might make your life extremely miserable.

The world is full of different people and knowing your way with around with them can easily become a determining factor in your pursuit of becoming a millionaire.

Keep reinventing yourself

Reinventing oneself has been a purifying ability which has been taught centuries ago from one generation to another.

It's important to reinvent yourself because by reinventing yourself you recreate yourself by rising from the ashes to become stronger, wiser, smarter and better than before. We all have phases in our lives where our creative power just fades away and we become bleak shadows of what we used to be. As we enter those phases, we need to be reborn in order to spring to action and become more productive, creating new things and inspiring others.

We often slip away in the state of degradation where we aren't living up to our full potential. The worst thing about it, is that usually we hardly even notice it.

One of the most successful movie directors, Michael Bay once noted:

"What I look for in a script is something that challenges me, something that breaks new ground, something that allows me to flex my director muscle. You have got to think fast in this business,

you've got to keep reinventing yourself to stay on top."

So in other words you need to show effort to reinvent yourself and you need to do it continuously and in some cases very frequently. Now why would you need continuous or even frequent self-reinvention? It's because sometimes we drift in so called comfort zone and get stuck there for longer periods of time or get off balance emotionally and mentally, which in its turn impairs our capability to produce creative content in our lives. As you become so to say reborn and start thinking in a new way or in an enhanced way compared to your previous self, you will notice how things start changing. You might take a new direction in your life or set your priorities differently. It's like you are a new plant which is growing from the roots towards the sun, powered with awe inspiring motivation.

By reinventing yourself, you will notice how the path you previously were walking on might be wrong way altogether. You also might suddenly figure out solutions to the problems you had prior to your self-reinvention.

Using the analogy of acting, you can become a new character and let the world be a stage for you. Anything is possible and all the doors are open for those who have full confidence in their new roles. With some imagination you can picture and visualise a different you. Sometimes it just snaps all of a sudden and you find yourself in a different body with a different mind. Your own conscious self-awareness directs you towards the decisions you make in your life.

Commit fully to what you do

No matter what your activities are, the most positive results are usually achieved when you commit fully to what you do. In case of a longer project, full commitment on your part becomes a critical factor in order to reach your goal and achieve success.

Healthy commitment is based on foundation of a few building blocks of 3 D:s. Those blocks are:

- Determination
- Diligence
- Discipline

Determination essentially represents your decision to finish what you started in spite of what happens along the way. Diligence, on the other hand, means being loyal and hardworking. Discipline means harnessing your willpower to keep you in line doing what's productive and necessary.

By having this kind of mindset, you will be able to achieve much better results. By committing to your projects you culminate every bit of your energy and attention to what needs to be done. Part of you might fight against you, while you're trying to build something great, but you need to harness your energy and your progressive values in order to keep achieving results frequently. It's not easy. Sometimes it might feel like you're rolling a gigantic stone up the hill everyday from morning until night. No matter how difficult and tiring it might feel like, you can always get extra strength and motivation by realizing the importance of what you are doing. This way, no matter how big or heavy the boulders might seem, you'll just keep on pushing.

You are responsible to yourself and possibly other people for your success. This creates a sufficient reason to commit 100% to what you are doing. You shouldn't focus on modifying the smallest details of your work with a microscope, unless that's the nature of your work, because playing with the details leads to perfectionism and stalls your work.

Understand the idea of constantly making profit

It's hard for some people to fundamentally understand just how essential it is to keep the idea of profiting at the epicentre of your life. The truth is, what you cherish the most and what you think of the most, often ends up increasing quantitatively in your life.

If you can wake up with the clear idea of how you can make more profit today and have the sense of urgency and eagerness to it, then you're definitely on the right track. On the other hand, if you think that profiting can wait, then what do you think is going to happen? It's like you tell an important person who has a an opportunity for you to wait on your door step. After making that person wait for 1 hour, you might notice that the person you asked to wait for you might no longer be there. So set profiting as your top priority. It should comprise everything that can definitely or potentially bring you profit. The more profit something or someone can bring you, the higher value you should assign to it.

Imagine that you are an accountant who is reviewing balance sheets during a severe economic depression. You are going through countless of balance sheets. Most of the numbers are negative at the bottom of the sheet. The companies are not making profit, they are losing money. Now imagine being the CEO of that company.

It's not impossible to prevent yourself from generating loss at all times. If you prioritize profiting, you will go to extraordinary lengths to insure you are profiting. You spend less or you change your suppliers for example. There are many tactics and strategies you can use to reach profitability no matter what your trade is. It takes ambition. It takes determination. It's a culmination point of a character who does not want to give up or let anything or anyone stay on his way to make profit. For some people this might sound harsh, but it's like a competition, where you can either win or lose. You choose to win and you don't give yourself an option to lose.

Believe in yourself

Believe in yourself! Have faith in your abilities! Without a humble, but reasonable confidence in your own powers you cannot be successful or happy.

- *Norman Vincent Peale*

This is probably the one of the most important steps in this chapter. You must have confidence in yourself. It takes only one person to believe in yourself and that person is you.

You might have been born to this world from your mother's womb and you might be enjoying the comfort of your friends and family, not to mention the loved ones, but as an individual you are a single person that needs to make things happen. But if you want to be successful, you must start believing that you will be. To believe that you can walk the walk and be successful because it's what you were born to do!

There are many stock brokers there, who's key to success is believing in their skills, believing in their knowledge that they have gathered and fundamentally believing in their intuition. They have to make split second decisions that only come out of strong belief in themselves. Of course they also need all the necessary skills, but without self-belief they might be too insecure or nervous to be able to achieve success.

Some things in the world are incredible and completion of many plans is improbable. It takes strong belief to overcome the impossible and do the unthinkable.

Believing in unison with others

When you start believing in something together with other people, your own belief strengthens. And the more people you got believing in the same cause, the better for you. If you have people in your team who ware creating a new innovation and all of you believe in its success, even though there's no guarantee that there will be any success, the probability of that success adds up by each and every member who believes.

Sometimes other people might judge your efforts or think that you will never be able to accomplish what you dream of accomplishing. That's when it's more important than ever to keep believing. Just cling to your belief and don't listen to those who are just there to criticize you without providing any useful word of advice in the process.

One of the presidents of the United States, Theodore Roosevelt, once said:

"Believe you can and you're halfway there."

That's a powerful statement and you should always remember it. Whenever you are unsure of whether you're going to make it, you will remember those words and keep on going.

Learn from yesterday– Focus on today – Build for tomorrow

Sometime life seems to be like a rollercoaster. Many of us don't simply have the discipline to do what's right. It all depends on how you look at your life, the world and the people around you.

Sustainable success pattern

There's a one easy pattern that really boosts your chances of achieving a real success, quantifiable in millions of dollars. Actually there is no cap on how much money you can make or how many other dreams you can turn into reality if you just follow one simple pattern: "Learn from yesterday (the past) – Focus on today (live in the moment) – Build for tomorrow (the future)". That's what I call a sustainable success pattern.

There's over 7 billion people living on earth. All of them are different from each other in many ways and one of those differences is their philosophy.

Some of us live in the past. Especially the older generations tend to play their mantra of: "I wish I was young again" or "The old times were best". This type of emotional setting will lead to depression. So don't live in past, the past is gone. There's nothing valuable for you in the past, except for lessons learned.

Some of us live in the future. Many different feelings might be associated with the future, like neofobia; in other words fear of the future. Some people, on the other hand, just wait and wait for a big change in their lives when everything just turns great for them. They will fall in love with someone perfect, they will find a great job with the highest salary ever and so on. This is just a fantasy illusion. Keep dreaming if you don't want to take responsibility of your life and achieve success. Success is for those who stand firmly in "today".

Peaking beyond the horizon of future

However, in terms of pioneering, creating a completely new way of making money or creating a new technology requires peaking beyond the horizon of the future, but nevertheless even if that's the case, you need to be aware of what processes need to be planned, started and maintained in order to turn that vision into money making reality.

Even if you are unsure of what future might bring you, just live for today because no matter what you do, all doors will be opened for you if you wake up with thoughts like "Today, I will focus on today and do my best today". By avoiding the pitfalls of the past you also build a brighter tomorrow for yourself without you even noticing it.

Your future projections need to be like taking quick peaks at the navigator while you're driving. If you only keep staring at your navigator, you will probably crash. As in real life, if you just stare at the future without taking action, you will lose your drive power.

Move out of your comfort zone

Too much comfort isn't good for you. It makes you lazy, dull and unproductive. All the big decisions are made in the discomfort zone. That's where you need to settle down, but don't get me wrong. Comfort zone is important place to visit just to cool off and regenerate your batteries in. However, don't stay there for too long, or you will once again consumed by laziness.

If you have some professional responsibilities that you carry out independently like a company, you *are* the company. So why do you spend time watching TV late at night, when you could get some valuable sleep in order to be fresh and sharp in the morning?

Every minute that you waste is the price you pay at the end of the day. Every bit of creativity that you destroy in the comfort zone will cost you 10 times more to regain in the discomfort zone. So grow a spirit of a fighter and toughen up because it's a tough world out there.

Grow a spirit of a fighter

What is a spirit of fighter? Many fighters and warriors went to battles for thousands of years, with an attitude that reflected fearlessness, motivation and self-assurance. During their battle campaigns they had to sleep in tents and live in harsh conditions.

You and me, on the other hand, are surrounded by all kind of electronic devices that only increase the risk of us becoming utterly lazy. In many countries there's a wonderful welfare system. But it's not for them who are capable of working. Those who get benefits while being fit to work are losers. In the old days people would work relentlessly. Just roll up your sleeves and build your fortune. The real Spirit of a Fighter reflects a high level of power of will. Make a decision to focus only on making profit and that's it. Dedicate yourself 100% to building your revenue like it's a do or die –case. If you follow this path, you will soon see the results.

You could do a following test: Each time you browse the Internet or watch TV for no apparent reason, set a timer to calculate how much time has elapsed from beginning of these activities to their completion. How much do you think wasting your time on a daily basis increases your productivity? Many great money makers out there don't spend their time like that, waiting for success to take them by surprise because they have all their focus on building their wealth. They work their way towards the success. If wasting your time is your habit, then you are either lazy or addicted to some form of activity that produces no productive output whatsoever.

Getting rich is not supposed to be simple. You need a lot of mental and physical energy. If you think life is supposed to be easy and fair while you are low on your finances, then you thought wrong, pal. I recommend that you watch a movie called: "Glengarry Glenn Ross", where the character, played by Alec Baldwin, delivers a powerful message to the real estate brokers: "ALWAYS BE CLOSING".

Understand the concept of money

Money is material, which you use to purchase something. It can be means to an end or it can be object of obsession. Either way we need money to be able to survive in this world. People who don't have enough money must struggle to survive. Nobody likes the piling up bills, empty fridges, nothing to brag with to the neighbours. When your child goes to school wearing rags, his class mates start bullying him because he dresses up like a poor kid, how would it make you feel? Furthermore, material problems can destroy your health and relationships. You must not let that happen.

Is it bad to be rich?

Many of us have been educated by the morals, which state that the richest of us are greedy and vicious individuals. But what if they have gathered their fortune through hard work?

My point is: Many of us have a barrier in our subconscious which prevents us to strive for excessive wealth.

Why should you feel bad about acquiring that excessive wealth? After all, you are returning more money to the society by paying more taxes than the average Joe! So why should you be sorry for being rich? And if you have your heart in the right place, you will be giving some of your money away for charity. Many wealthy people have done so and haven't regretted about that. In fact, many of those who have contributed their money for charity purposes, have done so repeatedly.

Money makes the world go around

The money really makes many things simpler both in your private life and when it comes to various things on a much larger scale. There is a saying, which states that: “Money follows the money”. Well what does that mean? It means that those who have already make a lot of money will more likely be getting richer, when the poor and average folks don’t. Your first 1 million dollars will be your toughest to achieve, but the second one will be much easier to make.

If money would grow on trees or if we could just print our own currency, the world would be a very different place. It’s so easy to spend money, but on the contrast, it’s challenging to make money. Our determination, creativity, wits and relentless persistence can lead to acquiring a lot of money.

Your attitude towards money makes a difference

Your money attitude, in other words how you look at the money actually affects on what are your probabilities of having more of it. If you see the money just as a tool for spending then that’s what it’s going to be for you, but on the other hand if you set earned money as your goal, the result might be drastically different.

Your best bet is letting the money be the output of you following your heart and doing something that you love. Many people have gotten rich by doing something that they were meant to do in the first place.

CHAPTER 2

Practical principles

Here I have listed the most essential practical principles

You will need to stick to them if you truly want to achieve great financial fortune.

Build a strategy

Building a proper strategy is an important way of paving your way towards success. Building a strategy is quite simple.

The first steps

Firstly, you need to commence something which is called the situation analysis. That means collecting information on your current situation. Also you need to analyze your strengths and find out what your weaknesses are. Also, think of what external threats and opportunities you are currently facing.

Build your master plan

Secondly, you need to plan what you can do to get rich. When you have chosen your plan, a master plan so to say, it's time to build blueprints for it and start gathering all the necessary raw materials like equipment and starting to turning your dream into reality. It gives you a great feeling watching your plan turn into reality. You can always introduce your project to your close friends and ask them for their opinions on it.

If you are working on an ongoing process, then it's monitoring is essential. By monitoring I mean supervising and overseeing the functions that might for example be automated, outsourced or run by your employees. This way you will ensure that everything is going according to your plans and you will be able to react to the possible problems much quicker. Forming a strategy is very easy

Seize the opportunities

Your big opportunity may be right where you are now.

- *Napoleon Hill*

You probably know what opportunity means. It's a chance to get what you want. Let me tell you a story.

Once upon a time there was a young woman, who worked in New York as a hair dresser. One day she was walking on the busy streets of New York. When she was crossing a street, a world famous film director Luc Besson happened to notice her. After that she was approached by the assistant of Luc Besson, giving her his business card and asking her if she would like to meet him. That was opportunity number one. So they met and in the process she was given another opportunity: To study acting for a few months in order to possibly get a film role. After that she was chosen to play a key role Transporter 3 blockbuster movie. The actress was Natalya Rudakova and her acting career continues. She has become a wonderful actress.

In this chapter I will teach you how to see an opportunity and grab it by its horns. It's a major part of millionaire mindset.

The Eldorado of hidden opportunities

I call the Internet an Eldorado of hidden opportunities and you know why? Because anyone can make money online. In many cases you don't even need to have a degree. You just need to use your wits to push yourself through the gateways of opportunity. Never think that you won't be able to live up to the requirements of the opportunity. You want to become a famous pop singer? You want to become a Hollywood actor? You want to become an astronaut? Go for it!

The only thing you can regret more than a failure is a missed opportunity. You probably have a computer and internet access. Now close your eyes and think hard of what you want to be. Pick a career path and type in the search engine: "how to become ...(your career choice)". In a few minutes you will already know various ways of how to become what you want to become. Now learn all about it and start taking action by pursuing it.

However, nothing guarantees that you will succeed. You need to narrow down your actions and determine the steps. I'm here to get you mentally prepared. I'm your trainer. No matter what your trade will be, you can be successful at it. Just make sure you keep looking for the right opportunities to shine.

Don't put it off for later

Never postpone taking an opportunity. You will need to investigate your opportunity thoroughly first, but if you have no reason to put it off, just go for it. You might regret your inaction, when the opportunity is no longer up for grabs.

Even if you are a slow starter, you should act when the time is right. The opportunity could be your pot of gold at the end of the rainbow, but make sure to find out all about it before you commit to it, or it might be your pitfall.

Be proactive

Being proactive means doing a lot of necessary things in advance in order to enhance the ongoing process or production that creates you profit. Being proactive can also be part of risk management. It is seeing the possible icebergs ahead and taking the necessary actions for your ship to be better prepared for them.

Now that you know the basic outlines of what being proactive actually means, we can get into the fundamental ways you can increase your level of proactive approach in many different areas.

First of all you have to be willing to think ahead. If you don't already have this tendency, you need to create a vision of possible future threats and opportunities and the ways you could react to them. The intensity of your proactive measures should be determined by the probability of those threats and opportunities. You should also expect the unexpected because often the odds are that anything could happen. You can't let yourself remain in full captivity of the present moment. You need to keep peeking in the future every now and then.

Here's what one of Great Britain's most legendary cricketers David Gower once said about a cricket team captain:

"He is a very positive captain; he is proactive as well as reactive. He is keen

to read the game, to get in there and he never stops thinking about the game, the situation and trying to turn it to his advantage. He has been very good for the game."

While we struggle and hustle to become as successful as we possibly can, we often need to be doing the same as the captain, described by Gower. Imagine that you are sitting in a control room. It's the command centre of your life. Your decisions have effect on even the smallest bits on your journey towards success. So all the proactive actions are within your reach to execute. The only questions are, when, where and how will you execute your proactive decisions.

By staying proactive, you can make distinct difference in your life. All your proactive decisions concerning your own life will affect the upcoming scenarios of your life. Sometimes you just have to take the initiative.

So what does taking the initiative really mean? It means taking the first step. Taking the first step towards achieving something, even though in some cases you might be somewhat unaware of the potential consequences. Your first step is like a stone that you cast in a lake. It creates multiple waves that, affect everything around the point of impact. Sometimes things just need to be done ahead of time. It's always better than just sitting and waiting for them to happen. That's how you intercept your success.

Keep it simple

Life is really simple, but we insist on making it complicated.

- *Confucius*

Oftentimes many people plan on constructing very complicated schemes to build their road to riches. This is why many of them fail at a very early stage. You need to keep things simple for yourself and for those who are working with you.

You really need to descend to the root level of your projects to be able to succeed at them. The multilayered organizational structures for example have been formed slowly and often during the course of several years and by the collective efforts of different people. Many billionaires have started out their companies from small garages and increased their production capacity over time. World class poker pros have mastered their skills little by little and moved from small games to more challenging ones.

No matter how complicated your trade is, you should keep your core process simple and cost efficient. Making things too complicated can simply lead to failure or burnout. If you can wrap your mind around all the necessary stuff that's required for you to get rich, then you will will definitely be able to stay energetic and productive throughout the entire course of your journey from the square one to being a millionaire.

Sometimes making things simple can be difficult. Steve Jobs once said:

“That's been one of my mantras - focus and simplicity. Simple can be harder than complex: You have to work hard to get your thinking clean to make it simple, but it's worth it in the end because once you get there, you can move mountains.”

Simplicity can also be applied to our everyday life. Here’s what Cary Grand had to say about it:

“My formula for living is quite simple. I get up in the morning and I go to bed at night. In between, I occupy myself as best I can.”

So we needn’t make our lives more difficult than they already are. By focusing on making things simple, we also get closer to achieving success. This is because simple things can be done faster and with better quality than difficult things, while using the same resources and capacities. Let’s close this chapter with the words of Arnold H. Glasow:

"Success is simple. Do what's right, the right way, at the right time.”

Find your perfect Niche

In the business world there are two things which you can sell: products and services. That's where the term Niche Market comes in.

If you sell shoes in a small town and you want to differentiate yourself from your competitors, you could sell the kind of shoes that nobody else around you is selling. Sports shoes for instance (in case there is no other sport shoe sellers in town except for you). There's also a lot niches blended in the wide range of sports shoes. You can start selling a specific type of sports shoes, like the shoes that are designed for running. Should this be the case, your best bet would be setting up a running shoe store in a town that doesn't already have one. When you advertise your company, make sure to specify your niche in the headline of your advert. Before you know it, you will be having plenty of customers.

Niches can be found in all the major areas of business. You should focus on the niche that represents something you are particularly interested about or have a great deal of knowledge of.

The best niches are brand new products or services that can give you a monopoly position. You will be the only supplier until new faces show up in the market. Sometimes you might need to collaborate with other people in order to create a unique niche.

A niche doesn't necessarily need to be a brand new product. It could be something that's already in the market. By modifying it, you create a different product.

So you want to be a niche player? Here's what Jim Oberweis says about niches:

"I think you have to be a niche player. You've got to find smaller ideas that are going to benefit in the conditions as they are. You can change the conditions and always try to find ways to make money in the conditions as they exist."

That's pretty straightforward, right? You don't need to wait for some magic wand to fall from the sky to give you special powers that allow you to create unique niches that would make you super wealthy. It's the small bits here and there that build up your income. Sometimes your niche can turn out to be a super star – niche. So if you stay on that path, sooner or later you will build your great fortune or team up with those who make it happen much faster.

Spot the demand and establish supply

Even though we live in the changing world, the rules of making money are fundamentally the same: find demand and establish supply. It's commonsense that if face low demand, you won't be earning a lot of money.

That's why you should find yourself a source of great demand and find a way to establish constant supply. Of course in real world things are not that simple. There are always other players in the playground of supply and demand. You need to show that you are better than your competitors to earn your place as the supplier. On the other hand, you should strive for spotting new areas of demand quickly enough and manage to establish a functioning chain of supply along with impeccable customer service, it might very well turn out to be a successful deal.

These days the world has become much smaller due to things like globalization, digitalization and modernization. We live in the age of internet, where countless amounts of online products are only a few clicks away. There are people in different parts of the world who want something. All you need to do, is to be within their reach. That is accomplished via marketing. Marketing can enhance the demand of your products and services to a great extent. You should strive for the scenario where there is balance between supply and demand.

Markets are the place where you can find demand and you are representing the supply. If there's too much supply in the market, so that demand doesn't meet the capacity of supply, then the markets are saturated. You should find out if some field of market is saturated with excess of supply, so that you know: that area isn't a good place to compete in.

Likewise, there can be excess in demand. Usually if the local markets don't have supply available, the supply is being brought from overseas. You can always compete with cheaper prices and better quality, but hardly against the well established multinational brands. Look for demand little by little, get one client at a time and sooner or later you might become that gigantic well established brand.

Think globally

These days we seem to have abundance of everything in developed countries. However, the developing countries, especially rapidly developing countries like China or Brazil have plenty of space for new businesses that are commonplace in the fully developed markets of the western world. Also, this doesn't rule out the fact that that the changing world always creates new demand. The aging baby boomers for example create increase demand of healthcare services. The digitalization, on the other hand, creates increasing demand for programmers and so on.

The globalization has given us the opportunity to think globally. It has given us the opportunity to reach outside the borders of our native countries and that's often a factor that can even turn a millionaire into a billionaire. Imagine a product or a skill that is widely common in your own country. Now imagine that if you establish a commercial foothold in a place like Hong Kong, your revenue could skyrocket within a short period of time. Hong Kong is a great example because it offers a great marketplace for wide range of businesses and has a favourable taxation policy.

Thinking globally does not only mean spotting the regional opportunities, but also being aware of the risks of new markets. The risks could translate into political or economical volatility for example. In essence, political volatility means local conflicts in different areas of the world for example. Such conflicts could be wars or regimes that cause more or less difficulties for foreign businesses to enter the local market and maintain their business operations. Economical volatility, on the other hand, means an economical environment that is very vulnerable to changes.

Seasoned entrepreneurs know that it's important to expand your business to more fruitful plains, where there is a lot more demand and space for growth. In such places the growth can be very rapid. There isn't a list of countries where you will need to start your business at to become a millionaire, it just doesn't work that way. Instead, for each market you enter, there are different locations on national and global scale that would be a great kick starter field for your business or an excellent platform for a growing business. Foreign markets often have much more space for different industries, perhaps even the industry that you are specialized in.

When entering a foreign market at the kick-start stage of your business, the first priority is to get all the support from the local governance you can get. It goes without saying that financial support is one of your top things on your "to do" – list. In other words, you need someone to invest in your company. If a government wants to invest in your company and support it in other ways, it's almost like a jackpot for you. As long as you have the majority of shares to your own company, you are in control.

Alternatively, you can find a local investor within the local investment organizations. Remember, that your operations overseas must be in full compliance with the local law. You can look up all the information on the internet or ask legal advice from one of the local lawyers.

On individual level, entering a foreign market could mean relocation to another country and facing the local cultural differences that could be shocking at first. Alternatively, if you have already formed a prominent business in your home country, you could form partnership with a local business and let them represent you overseas. You could form a franchising contract between you and that company and watch seeing your business grow overseas.

Generate wealth from your values

There is a form of wealth which less and less people seem to generate. It's the inner wealth, the inner richness. What do I mean by this? I mean living in line with your morals, keeping your conscious clean, setting an example for those who see you and those who don't. This is what I call the inner wealth.

I'm going to talk about the benefits of having great values. If your value is honesty and integrity, then you will not only attract other people, you will also attract potential customers and have a great chance to convert them into buyers. People appreciate those who have great values.

On the other hand, if you follow the egocentric trend of our modern society and just do whatever you can to get rich: lie, backstab, threaten, steal or do something else that's morally questionable, then you obviously don't have any inner wealth and the material wealth will always seem to be insufficient or slip through your fingers leaving you miserable.

Success *comes to those who practise good values.* You might also hear a sports commentator say a sentence about a professional athlete, like: "She had a lot of heart". It's not just passion. It's a mix of passion, values and commitment. Old stories or song lyrics might say: "Listen to your heart". It is a wise message. Follow the righteous path and to do what you feel that is right.

It's not a coincidence that many companies have dedicated an entire page under the headline of " Our Values" on their website. Deep inside each of us wants to live by good moral values and on certain level we can appreciate it in others whether they are individuals or businesses.

As humans, we are interesting and complex beings. If we are true to our values, just giving some of your wealth back to society results in burst of energy and ecstatic feelings. Values are something that unify us all from around the world.

When it comes to becoming rich through your values, remember that if you have great values, you are not only representing yourself, but also your values. By representing your values, your values will represent you. That will make you more energetic, valuable, inspired and dedicated. You can focus on what you are doing without any moral issues haunting you because your values are on your side and you can proudly do what you do. The world is open for you and you can reach the stars if you want.

Although it’s good to be modest, you should state your values on your CV or website. Somewhere where people can see them, but when you do state them, do not just act like they are just meaningless statements. Make sure that you actually *show* your values in your everyday life having them as default features of what you represent.

Your values could lead you to some amazing opportunities or deals that you could never have achieved if your values weren’t there to make you worthy of those things. Good things happen to those who work hard and build their reputation. It’s like forging your own luck.

Fame equals money

Many people don't realize that fame and money are interconnected. Famous people tend to make more money because their fame works for them. They have employed their fame making money out of it. That's why so many famous and successful people do everything within their power to maintain an impeccable public image.

People are willing to pay to buy the CD's of established stars of the music industry, so they could brag to their friends showing them the CD's they purchased. Fame sells. Although you don't necessarily need to be famous in order to be super rich, your company commonly does. Something that you represent must be top listed and have great reviews. If you are a business owner, get some positive testimonials and post the best of them on your website. Also, if you have some of the top companies in the world as your clients, make sure to show it on your website as well.

Now let's look at an example of how you can take advantage of fame. Imagine becoming famous on YouTube. Imagine that your video is getting tens of millions of viewers. At that point there are a lot of people who are interested in you. If you find out that even celebrities or TV hosts are watching your video, you are not far from potentially signing a million dollar contract with a production company for instance. So if you ever find yourself in a situation like that, don't let the opportunity slip away, but take advantage of it when the hype is at its highest point. Expand your online presence and make yourself even more famous and available for those million dollar deals.

However, not everyone can handle the pressure of being famous. So if you want to achieve success through becoming famous, you better start getting mentally prepared for it. Never think that you aren't the right type for it. All the celebrities are humans just as you. You are just as suitable for it as anyone else in the world.

You can start developing your public image on different networking sites like Facebook and LinkedIn. Bring out the best of you. Do something cool and new, record it and then publish it on YouTube. If it goes viral, then both you and your video receive a lot of publicity. Just as the teen pop star Justin Bieber became famous on YouTube, you could become the new internet celebrity.

So start paving way for fame now. If you don't have profiles set up in social media, do it now. Even if you would be applying for job, your recruiters will probably try to look you up on a search engine. It's an internet image that create for yourself. It's something that makes you sort of like a brand. So let's assume that you are a brand. Then you should definitely use all your efforts to maximize the positive impression people get when they are viewing your profile. Even if you launch a new product or a service, it needs to have internet representation to enhance its fame. Internet and social media in particular are the best ways to advertise your internet presence.

Right now, you can check the current state of your internet presence: Type your name in Google search engine, or alternatively type the name of your company. Check how many results you get. You can check the amount of results on the top left corner of your browser after your search. The more results there are, the better. And remember: Even negative fame isn't always as bad as it seems. In some cases it might actually turn out to be a good thing for your business.

Learn to productise anything

Everything in this world has its value and even though many say that some things are invaluable and some things cannot be bought. However, most things can be productised.

From the economic point of view, many things that you have around yourself can be turned into profit making machines. For example if you have a spare room in your house, you can rent it out. If you speak a foreign language, you can tutor someone at your spare time and get paid for it. Note that these are just the primitive steps of how you can put a price tag on things that can end up being highly profitable in the long run. If you have a spare car, you could lease it out and so on.

When it comes to pricing, you need to evaluate the current market value of something you want to put a price tag on. If you are an independent broker, you need to value your commission properly so it won't scare your potential customers off. On the other hand your commission needs to be high enough so that you would remain profitable.

The skill of productising anything can be learned through experience. Start from simple things in a small scale and gradually move on to more challenging and profitable objects. Do you remember getting something in return for the goods or services that you provided as a kid? Perhaps you showed some tricks and asked for candy in return? That's already a basic form of productising. It doesn't get much more complicated than that. Just make sure that your product is valuable, consumer friendly and easily distributable. Those are the key points. If you happen to face demand, you will need to produce more of what you are currently producing. So are you able to productise something which could potentially end up being very much in demand?

A real businessman can handle productisation. It takes a lot of effort to turn any object or service into a product. Hundreds of years ago businessmen would stand in the middle of a street and sell a cure-all potion, bottled, labelled and trademarked. While it might not have been a cure-all at all, it gave the impression that it certainly was one. And large masses of people would buy. While this sort of unethical way of doing business can be morally questionable, it's certainly a great lesson for you. You can pull the same thing off, but within the moral framework of course.

Nowadays people seem to think that everything worth of inventing has already been invented and everything worth of productising has already been productised. Well, not everybody thinks that way. The true pioneers always keep trailblazing, inventing new stuff and productising new products. They smoothen down the rough terrain of robust market areas and pave the way for their competitors. They aren't afraid to put enough effort and resources in hope of generating profit. The pioneers who can also envision success, often do achieve it. It also takes a lot of experience and tries and failures to reach that stage where your productisation leads to success.

I would like you to imagine of any object or service you can think of. Now start planning a better version of it. You can do the same with any service you can think of. Plan all the characteristics, evaluate the production costs, calculate the breakeven point and the theoretical gross margin. Now create the prototype. Make sure that you retain the legal rights to your product or service. Do some market research and launch a marketing campaign. Establish a plan for scaling up the production. If there is demand you will start making profit and eventually will become a millionaire.

Turn your failures into success

Once upon a time, centuries ago, there was an inventor who lived in France and dreamed of creating a perpetual motion machine. He did create a round spinning object, but as a perpetual motion machine, it turned into a failure. This happened in 17th century France and the inventor was Blaise Pascal, who had invented Roulette, perhaps the most famous casino game in European history.

This was just one example how modifying failed project could lead to unimaginable success and not just in the field of inventing. Some people say that you must admit your failure. Some people break down after experiencing a failure. Well from now on your new motto will be: "Nothing motivates me more than a failure", but this doesn't mean that you need to strive for failure. You need to respond to it in the right way. if it occurs.

You must never let the failures to get under your skin. That might lead to severe depressions. Every failure is a unique learning opportunity. Your failures could make you realize that you had completely insufficient approach. With the burst of motivation you get from failure, you will modify your approach and get the job done the way it should be done in no time.

As a definition, failure is basically a result of not achieving your goal. It might be either your fault or someone else's fault. The point is, you didn't get what you wanted and that usually pisses people off. You need to keep your head clear and think, how you could turn this situation around in your favour.

It takes truly exceptional fighting spirit to try and look for the best in the worst case scenario. John D. Rockefeller once remarked:

"I always tried to turn every disaster into an opportunity."

What more is there to say? We live in an age, where there are so many people, that someone else can easily take advantage of the opportunity your failure possibly creates. Let's name it a rebound opportunity in basketball terms.

When a basketball player fails to score and the ball just bounces off the backboard, he might decide to grab the ball again and attempt to score again. How badly do you want to score? There are plenty of chances for a rebound points if you just observe circumstances of your failure closely enough.

Learn to work under pressure

Stress is prevalent in everyday life of working class heroes. If you want to become a self-made millionaire, pull up your sleeves, cause you will be sweating a lot. Where there is a high concentration of responsibility, there's also going to be a lot of pressure.

You probably know what gravity is. It's the force that pushes you down. Pressure often feels like increased gravity. Not only does it push you down, but it also squeezes you from every side and makes your heart rate go up. Excess pressure and high concentration of stress can result to psychological and physical problems if you can't handle pressure and stress to that extent. Your mind affects your body. It is the control centre of your arms, legs and other body parts. Your mind also affect your heart and other organs that are vulnerable to stress. I'm going to teach you some of the elementary basics of how to cope with pressure and prevent harmful stress.

Firstly, learn to accept the pressure. Don't fight it, but don't let it get control of you either. When you are under pressure, your body reacts to various stress signals. Sometimes you might feel the tension in your shoulders. This is when you should relax your shoulders and let them fall down, not too much though, but just enough to release the tension. This will make some of the pressure go away. At least for a while. Also, you should improve your work environment. If you work on a computer, you should have the screen fixed at your eyelevel and your elbows should rest on a table in a 90 degree angle when you are typing. Your back should be straight and your muscles relaxed.

Practice working in these conditions. No matter how high the pressure is, your mind will clear up if you can just relax. Most likely this will not come easily at first, but practice makes perfect. Eventually, when you will have a lot at stake, the ability to handle your stress by relaxing and thinking with a clear mind will often be the determining factor to your success rather than failure. It will also keep you healthier.

Pressure energy

When you are preparing for a competition, a certain amount of stress can enhance your competing capability in your competing environment.

Now we are going to discuss how to harness pressure to create extra energy for you to be able to achieve more and perform better. It's a commonly known fact that when you are performing in front of people, a small amount of pressure is good for you. Too much pressure results in excessive sweating, increased heart rate and sometimes the loss of consciousness. So take slight bits of pressure and turn them into your energy, so when you will be performing in front of a large crowd of people for instance, where each of the listeners will be paying thousands of dollars to hear you talk, you will get the best elements out of your own pressure to boost the quality of your performance.

Stress can be addicting and you can learn to enjoy the adrenaline rush flowing though your body. Just make sure that you stay in control of your stress so that stress doesn't take control over you.

Avoid taking debt

Many small business owners, students, newlyweds and other people think that the first step of building their future is taking a loan. They purchase whatever they want to buy and trust that someday they will pay the loan back. Unfortunately in only one thing is for certain. The debt needs to be paid back. Furthermore, the debt will grow in interest, which adds up to the total amount of liability. Never take your income for granted. Especially if you are about to take a huge loan.

Your debt is your liability in financial terms. It is your deficit. If you have to take debt make sure you take all the precautions to prepare yourself for the worst case scenario. Luckily though, all major debts have a collateral. The collateral of a real estate loan is the piece of real estate to be purchased.

But here's the good news. If you are planning to create a small business of your own, you don't need to take debt. Often all you need is an investment ranging between a few dollars and few thousands of dollars. There's a good chance you have that amount of money on your account and if you don't, try to negotiate a long term loan with your relatives or close friends before you even think of going to the bank.

There have been many super profitable businesses that started in a garage with little or no investment at all. There have been a lot of low budget blockbuster movies in the history of films. Archie Karas, a professional gambler, went to Las Vegas in the mid 90's with only 50 bucks in his pocket. In three years he turned those 50 dollars into 40 million dollars. This proves that you don't need to take loans or wait for investors decision in order to start making money.

Unless you are a banker, the word debt should associate with negative things that you don't want to have anything to do with. Debt often leads to major depression. Debt associates with debtors knocking on your door and taking your precious stuff. Instead of growing debt, you should focus on growing your self-sufficiency. Investors love buying stocks of a self-sufficient company. And when investors buy your stocks the value of price per share grows and your company makes more money. Self-sufficiency means that you are independent external financers. So aim for that.

Crowdfund instead of taking a loan

If you require funding and aren't quite sure where to go asking for money, you should try crowdfunding your venture. Crowdfunding is a relatively new way of raising money for different causes. If you present your idea in an appealing fashion and assign suitable perks for your sponsors, you could be generating a generous amount of capital for your business. Even though it sounds simple, building a successful crowdfunding campaign actually requires a lot of effort. The crowd consists of your possible investors who would be putting their own money to support your idea, so you better be convincing enough. You need to be able to make a great impression and to inspire the crowd.

Be patient

He that can have patience can have what he will.
- Benjamin Franklin

Patience is a virtue they say and even if it sounds like a cliché, It's actually a very important attribute to your efforts to reach success.

It takes time to achieve success

Imagine that you start a project that has high expectations. As the time goes by, you aren't seeing any results and you become depressed and willing to quit. Now visualize a plant that take time to grow its roots. The same thing applies to your plans where you want to become a millionaire. After a while, when the roots grow big enough, the plant starts growing quickly and produces fruits. It takes time to become successful and usually achieving grand success takes even more time.

Impatience can impair your health

Sometimes you get into a mood where you produce quickly, but the results that you expect from other interest groups are still pending. You grow impatient and often blame those interest groups for being incompetent. Bear in mind that impatience can lead to a major health risk. It most likely rises your blood pressure and can cause a heart attack, but that's just an example of the negative aspects that impatience can cause.

Recognize the pending processes

Impatience can also lead to bad results. Ultimately it can even deprive you of getting paid big bucks for something that just required a bit more patience. You should really learn how to recognize the pending processes. Let's assume that you are working on a project which is a "bigger fish" that will make you a ton of money upon its successful completion. Then on the other hand you have a lot of smaller projects or "smaller fishes" so to say. Let's assume that they take less time to accomplish and they have less pieces that need to be put together and they are easier to control altogether. Now imagine that the bigger fish is stalling. You've put your time and money to catch it, but it still isn't behaving as expected and can't do anything to fix the situation. So what do you do? Do you just dump it and move on or will you cling to it?

Well, in this case there is no right answer, simply because there are too many variables included. You can actually figure the answer yourself by looking at the calculations, trends, consulting with the right people and so on. Generally, being a bit more patient than you already are is a good thumb rule.

It's good to have plenty of patience, but don't let that affect your judgement. Sometimes it's good to be strict, especially if it's of utmost importance to get results within a tight schedule.

Copy the successful people

There's no need to reinvent the wheel if you can do the same thing as those people who made themselves millionaires. Just study what they did and do the same! There's plenty of free information about the rich and successful people online. You can even create a routine of spending an hour a day watching clips of documentaries and interviews of the richest people on YouTube or reading their biographies or blogs on a daily basis.

Read about their habits and copy them. Read about their investment strategies and do the same. Find out what they did when they started out with nothing. These days the new millionaires are emerging faster than ever before and a lot of them are from the developing countries. It's not the best plan to repeat the things people did hundreds of years ago to become wealthy, but rather the things people do these days.

Rags to riches

Many billionaires have made it from "rags to riches". Some of them grew up in an orphanage or came from a poor family. Some of them immigrated to the United States from relatively poor countries and worked at minimum wage jobs when they realized that they could set up their own companies. Many of them have changed the world as we know it and created brands that everyone knows.

Often those unforgettable tycoons have had massive breaks that paved the way for their real success. For example, Microsoft was still a relatively small company before an event which occurred when IBM made a deal with Microsoft. As a result, Microsoft started producing operation systems for IBM computers. Later on, Microsoft started producing its own standalone products that were widespread and the company achieved major success. That resulted in series of events and eventually lead to Bill Gates, the founder of Microsoft, becoming the richest man on the planet.

As simple as the concept of copying the pioneers of technology might seem, most people choose the comfort of their routines over trailblazing. This can be called lack of courage as well as lack of enthusiasm, but you, my dear reader, could be a different case. You could become the founder of a next Apple or the next Microsoft. Of course I'm speaking metaphorically and referring to a next massively successful company that will change the world as we know it and make you very rich.

Relentless persistence

There is no force on earth that can stop you from fulfilling your dream if you really put your heart into it. Sometimes the efforts the successful people put in their work are so incredible that it might feel extremely difficult to do the same. It is said that Thomas Edison slept for only 4 hours and worked the rest of the time. Could you do the same? Even nowadays nobody gets successful just overnight so you really need to put all your efforts on the line to achieve success. Often persistence translates into relentless overtime hours of productive work.

There are also other "millionaire qualities", many of which are mentioned and discussed broadly in this book. Many successful people have been asked, what's their secret to success or which quality they would prioritize as the key quality that brought them success. There have been multiple different answers as there is no universal key for success. All of the qualities that the successful people have mentioned, such as: persistence, excellent customer service or great time management, have been fundamental building blocks for the success of those particular people. And besides, they would have probably given a list of different qualities if they weren't asked to name only one of them: The main quality; The secret of success. So make sure you learn and harness all those qualities, use them and earn your own fortune.

Evolve on a daily basis

Every day you should be able to become something more of what you already are. Have you ever played the online role playing games? In case you haven't, the main aim in those games is to develop new skills and level up so you can become stronger, more intelligent, more dexterous and so on. So in short, the main purpose of those games is to enhance the traits of your character. You can do the exact same thing to yourself in real life.

Firstly, you've got to avoid degradation and degeneration. Walking on a linear path with regard to your skills and competences is also counterproductive. There are so many different ways you can take yourself to the next level every day and be better, smarter and stronger than yesterday. So how will you deal with a challenge like that? It's simple actually. All you need to do is to put some willpower into good use and show some effort to move on to the next level. Many of the most successful people, the richest people imaginable, have set personal evolution as their standard. Even if you have a natural talent and show incredible skills, you still need to keep evolving because someday someone just like you will show up and replace you. You have probably heard of Charles Darwin's theory of evolution. Whether you believe in his theory or not, as personalities we can still keep evolving on a regular basis.

This isn't something that applies to only us as humans. Thousands and thousands of companies are tirelessly researching new technology and developing their products. If you develop products, then you are trying to deliver something that represents you to market. Your product tells a story of your evolution level. If you are running an R&D team, you need to make sure that it's performing well enough to match your company's preferences, your company's level of evolution in order to achieve success.

One can also speak of evolution of consciousness, as Tom Robbins states:

"Our greatest human adventure is the evolution of consciousness. We are in this life to enlarge the soul, liberate the spirit and light up the brain."

And here's what Nikola Tesla once stated with regard to evolution:

"It is paradoxical, yet true, to say that the more we know, the more ignorant we become in the absolute sense, for it is only through enlightenment that we

become conscious of our limitations. Precisely one of the most gratifying results of intellectual evolution is the continuous opening up of new and greater prospects."

Work less, but be make more money – the profitable type of downshifting

Downshifting became the new trend in the 90's. The main idea of it was changing lifestyle full of stress, work and rat race into something more simple and relaxed. Personal life and relationship shifted to new priorities and working went down the priority ladder. While the aim of this trend was to help people achieve their immaterial goals, it didn't make them any richer. As we all know, financial freedom allows us to tackle those goals more efficiently.

So what is it that we need to make it happen? We need to create a customized form of downshifting and apply it in our lives to become more profitable and happier at the same time. Some might thing that this can't actually be accomplished. Well I tell you that it can and it's not even that difficult so keep reading!

Customize your downshifting

Firstly, focus on the things that stress you the most in your life. Is it your current work, your spouse or the rush hour on the road? All these things are something which you recognize as stress factors at a conscious level, but there are several other things that cause you stress on subconscious level as well. These things are the pieces of electronic equipment you are surrounded by. Electronic devices like TV, radio, game consoles and a large variety of everyday objects in the places where you spend a lot of time. The actually build up your stress and disrupt your concentration.

Stress less – profit more

What you need is less stress and more profit. Repeat out loud: "Stress less – profit more". When you work in a relaxed environment, you produce more creative and possibly profitable ideas and feel much better at the same time. Imagine working at a home office environment. Renting an apartment at a quiet location, turning it into an office where you could concentrate on working without any disruptions. Some place where your mind is settled only at working and you don't hear the blabber of your colleagues or your spouse. Place like that could be the perfect Zen garden for your productivity and creativity.

Following the same passage of ideas, you could make some adjustments in order to work less on a specific project and get more money from it in the same time. For instance let's look at an example where your client has placed an order for a large project for creating his website that you originally were to handle by yourself. What you can do is, you can find freelancers and cut the project to small pieces. One of your freelancers would carry out the web design, another would do another part of the project and so on. Cost efficient outsourcing is an essential part of profitable downshifting for entrepreneurs. This way you will have more time to focus on other project and you will finish faster.

The quickest path to riches is mostly full of risks and pressure

One day you might wake up with an idea like: "I've fed up with being poor. I want become a millionaire!" This is the type of idea that many of the millionaires had back in the days when they didn't have much money. That was the time before they became rich. If you had one of those ideas or attitude changes, you should consider yourself fortunate because that might just be the spark that sets for the path of becoming rich.

Becoming rich quickly

A few words of warning though. As it states in the headline of this chapter, becoming rich quickly can bring a lot of risk and pressure upon you. This path can descend you to the lowest lows, but also bring you a fortune of a calibre that you never could imagine. There are many ways to make a lot of money fast, but there are also many ways to lose a lot of money fast. If you want to bet big in this game, make sure you have what it takes to deal with unimaginable losses.

I'll be absolutely clear with you: Unless you're lucky enough to win a jackpot in lottery or happen or have millions waiting just to be inherited by you, becoming rich will require you to deal with enormous risks and that already is enough to build a lot of pressure on your shoulders. I'm not going to suggest committing any criminal activity, such as robbing a bank or any other illegal activities due to moral and ethical reasons. There are, however a few legitimate ways to build your capital fast.

Stock market shark

Many people have made millions in only one year in stock market just by betting right. These people truly deserve the title of a stock market shark. You could also build a an investment company that deals with hedge funds. Then you would have to prove yourself to the prominent clients, not to mention mastering your trade and knowledge of the stock market before you set your foot on that path. On the other hand, if can raise enough capital, get a loan for instance, you could invest a ton of money if you can deal with the risk of a possibility of losing that money. Foreign exchange is also a great investment environment. You will want to go where there's more volatility. The most rapid changes in some particular stocks or currencies can bring the best profit fast. What you need is a sense for money. You need to have a deep understanding of the places that the big amounts of money are being circulated. Find a way to get inside those places and start making some quick money. Keep in mind that you might lose all you've got and even more. It's a game of tough players and if you have the guts, wits and nerves to play that game, you might have a good shot at making it big there.

And finally, any trade with quickly established high demand, accompanied by your ability to provide sufficient supply and of course your capability to scale things up quickly can earn you the status of a millionaire in a relatively short period of time. So dig deep and discover, which way is the one that's the most probable to grant you a fortune.

Cut down your spending

Wasting money is easy, making it is not that easy. Keep it in your head. Your money is like your dear friend. If you don't take care of it or you treat it with ignorance, someday it just might not be there for you anymore. It might turn into your enemy with a different name, called "debt" and debt isn't something that you want to have in your life.

If you are at home now, take a trip to your kitchen. When you arrive at your kitchen, open your fridge and see what's inside. As we all can imagine, you will find more or less products that represent beverages or food. Now find a product that has been in your fridge for several days, weeks or months even. In fact, it might even stay there for years unless it ends its journey in your trash can.

In fact some the products and services that you have spent money on are the ones you don't actually even need. Take a good look around you. That magazine or newspaper that's on the table, why would you order something like that, when you can read it online for free? Also your gym workout can be replaced by cost efficient home workout. If you don't live and work in a rural area, you don't need a car. You can use your feet, bike or a commuter. Take a look at your electricity deal. Are you sure that that's the cheapest one?

So many people are focusing on building their revenue, but what they really should focus on is cutting their expenses. Often when you scramble mindlessly for more money, working longer hours, you're actually making it worse. You will spend more money on doctors, treatment like drugs and therapy. By cutting your costs you can actually enjoy your life more. Even though most of the rich people seem to be enjoying their lavish lifestyle, it often doesn't contribute to their happiness. What does make them happiest is often the process of making money. If you get wealthier, you shouldn't automatically start spending all your money. It could be a tool for investments and other means of preserving your financial independence. The more money you have, the more liquid assets you have on your hands. Those assets can be used to make more money through buying shares or real estate. If you decide to buy something. Then buy something that will bring sustainable benefit in the long run.

Surround yourself by the right people

The headline says it all. Try to be around successful people as much as possible. If it's physically impossible to surround yourself with those people, hang out with them on the internet. Ask for their advice. Go and read some of their books.

Have you ever been at a baseball game where one of the players is obviously the most skilled player of all the players? People get inspired by great talents and often want to idolize great people. Nevertheless anyone can become successful starting from the square one. Just get inspired by the great people who have found their success. Feed your own motivation and mindset on their energy, skills and knowledge. Make them work for your benefit as your allies.

The fact is you are surrounded by people who affect you. In general they might not even affect you negatively, but their effect on you could contribute to you remaining in your current situation without willing to grow. They might be discouraging you from taking calculated risks in order to achieve wealth. You need the right kind of company. However, by saying this, I do not encourage you to dump all the people around you, just start finding some successful people and spending more time with them or talking with them via e-mail or instant messenger.

If you can't find any successful friends to inspire and consult you, you could join an online forum, where people discuss wealth and the ways to achieve it. By interacting with successful people online or by just reading their posts, you will realize on a conscious level that making a lot of money isn't extremely hard. You can even send private messages to successful people, this might start a very promising business collaboration. In other words, mingle with the rich!

There are many conventions where many successful people tell you about their experiences and the people attending those conventions are those, whom you should definitely add to your network. After all, It's much more probable for you to achieve success together with other likeminded people than all by yourself.

Think of it this way: You might need help to achieve value for yourself, but to get help you need to offer your helpers some value.

If on the other hand, if you surround yourself by people who undermine the value of money and want to live ordinary low paid life telling you how bad the rich people are, it will be very difficult for you to become a millionaire. If everyone around you is going to be talking about ordinary stuff and telling how evil, vicious and greedy the rich people are, you're going to end up just like them, unless you get out of their reach!

Be original

If you want to be like the super successful people, you need to learn how to do everything under your own headline. When you think of a business idea or a way to create a new service or existing one, you need to differ from your competitors substantially. *You need to be yourself.* Evaluate what your strengths are and try to work on your weaknesses. If you learn to enjoy creating something that pays, success won't be that far away.

It is hard for anyone to be original and creative, if you're dependant on something or someone or you are working under strict supervision of your employer. Originality is your trademark, something that your future customers will love you for. People want to see and experience something new because new is interesting and exciting.

By creating original idea you will also intrigue the investors. Be your own boss and don't look up to anyone when you are creating someone new. Some people might think that all the great brands are already created and there nothing new left to be created. That's rubbish. There's thousands of new ways to personalize your own success story. You can take bits and pieces from around of your personal life and form a trademark out of it.

There are tons of ways to make profit out of your own creation. The key is to keep your eyes open to the new ways *monetizing* your product.

There's not a lot of originality in crafting your own millions and its often not even that thrilling as you might think. It's just finding ways to generate money in large portions sustainably until there's seven digits on your bank account.

Every internet domain or a company name is original representation. You should never see the originality of your approach as a barrier. Let your originality be your asset.

Your originality can be influenced by famous brands out there. It doesn't have to be like straight from the planet Mars. You decide the originality level of your creation.

Bob Seger once said:

"Be original. That's my best advice. You're going to find that there's something that you do well and try to do it with as much originality as you can."

Always have a backup plan

You can't always predict how things will go. That's why it's good to have a backup plan or many different backup plans at your disposal.

Even if everything went according to your plans, you should always be prepared for the worst case scenario. It's critical to be prepared because things can get nasty if you encounter serious pitfalls while not having a backup plan. Lack of a backup plan can be both expensive and mentally devastating.

So here's a few easy guidelines for tailoring a backup plan for any kind of process: Firstly, imagine the worst case scenario. Be completely realistic and use your imagination. When you come up with an answer that makes sense to you, write it down on paper. Now think of few other negative outcomes, let say 5 of them. Write every single of those 5 possible scenarios, each on a separate line. Now start thinking for an antidote for each of those scenarios. Write them down next to each of the five theoretical negative projections that you already have written down. Now you should start thinking how to actually acquire those antidotes and what their cost would be. Perhaps you can acquire them in advance as a precaution? Many buildings and boats have fire extinguishers installed and ready for usage, even though there has never been a fire hazard. Be prepared, be smart, have a backup plan.

Exceed everyone's expectations

It's better to do something valuable in excess than do too little. You can never really overcontribute. There's lots of ways you can add value to your projects. You can study, plan, execute, develop, monitor and so on. Some people don't realize just how much effort they need to show especially during the first few weeks of their start-up activity to be successful. You need to be working with your hands and your brain and you need to be working a lot.

Just as every teacher loves a student who exceeds expectations, every employer loves an employee who exceeds expectations and that is likely to lead to great recommendations. A leader who lets his crew watch as he works exceeding expectations will be respected by his crew and set an example for it.

If you only deliver what is expected of you, you will not shine. You will be just another tool in the box. You need to think outside of the box, put your mind to it and start exceeding the expectations. Farrah Gray was a millionaire by the age of 14. He wouldn't have been a millionaire if he'd just think and act like a regular teenager. He exceeded the expectations of many and still keeps amazing and inspiring a lot of people from around the world today.

The point of this chapter is to make you understand that not only can you exceed the expectations that other people set on your performance, but you can also outperform your own expectations. Just follow the pattern below:

Keep Track of Your Expenses and Profit

Have you ever noticed how your expenses tend to build up, leading to a very unpleasant result that shows on your bank account? That's because you are not concerned enough about keeping track of your money. From there on out it gets much more natural for you to build up your profit and how to decrease your expenses.

There are some easy things you can do to keep track of your budget. You can create a balance sheet by using spreadsheet software on your computer or alternatively you can write it down on a piece of paper and stick it on your fridge for example. By documenting your personal financial data, you'll soon start to realize just how unnecessary some of your expenses are. And that may very well lead to effective expense cutting on your behalf. On the other hand, you'll pursue profiting much more eagerly. Think of yourself as a business – a profitable business.

Here's an example of how you can document your expenses:

Week 24	Monday	Tuesday	Wednesday	Thursday	Friday
Expense A (shopping) *	(-)20$				100$
Expense B (investment)**	(-)100$		(-)150$		200$
Total	**120$**				**300$**
Income	350$	200$	400$	300$	150$
Profit margin	**230$**	**200$**	**250$**	**300$**	**(-)150$**

Weekly total: **580$**

*Expense A is sheer liability

**Expense B potentially brings income later on as an investment

Saving

In the long run, the more money you save, the more you will accumulate. Things like currency value get decreased due to inflation or changes in the currency market. You can fight the devaluation of your capital by investing your money.

There are many people out there who make truckloads of money, but they simply can't handle their income. They always seem to be broke. The reason for that might be their readings on a so called financial thermostat.

Financial thermostat

Financial thermostat is not a physical object. It represents your ability to keep your overall capital at a certain level. It might sound silly, but many people just can't handle more than a certain amount of money on their bank accounts. The so called excess capital ends up as alcoholic liquid pouring down their throats or some form of other entertainment or perhaps a piece of furniture or a piece of electronic consumer technology that ends up being useless. That's why you should turn up the heat on your financial thermostat, in other words have more endurance holding more capital on your bank account without spending it on useless junk. As your thermostat values go up, you will notice just how easy it is to have money flowing into your account without simultaneously having the urge to spend it. Money no longer burns holes in your pockets and you can just keep it there or invest it making even more money in the process.

Dress for success

Clothes make the man. Naked people have little or no influence on society.

- *Mark Twain*

I want to tell you a little secret. Those who dress up well, are usually more successful financially than those, who dress up in torn jeans and a dirty T-Shirt. Therefore dressing for success is not an overstatement. Those who dress well, tend to be more confident in themselves on average. Increased confidence often results in increased productivity and revenue.

When you dress up like you mean business, you will not only make yourself appear more serious, but other people will also be taking you more seriously. Walk your way to success looking good, well dressed and your head held high because you deserve your success! It doesn't mean that you should wear the best stuff you can find. You don't need to always wear a suit and tie to feel important. Just wear tidy clothes that represent what you are all about.

Dressing up well doesn't necessarily mean that you need to spend a lot of money on clothes. All you need to do is purchase the clothes that suit you and boost your self esteem. That's when things start changing. You will start feeling better and more prone to achieving success.

No matter whether you are man or woman, a young or a senior person, you can always switch for the clothes that make you feel more confident, unless that's already your habit. Dressing up could substantially affect your efforts to reach success.

Learn New Skills

The importance of learning new skills can never be stressed enough. As a job seeker you are competing against the ever increasing number of other applicants. As a business owner you are competing not only against other companies, but also the growing amount of freelancers, who are in many cases basically stealing your potential customers, by offering lower prices and faster delivery times. Even in the world of professional poker players, the availability of free internet based strategies has been increasing the number of high level poker pros rapidly since the online poker boom in 2003.

Benefits of learning new skills

Learning new skills is very beneficial because it adds value to you and your skill portfolio. You can never have too many skills, while you certainly can be under-skilled. You see sometimes you just need to learn new skills to be able to produce value for others. Learning new skills can turn into a fun and exhilarating experience that you might remember for the rest of your life.

Learning new skills can also be beneficial for your health. For example, scientific studies show that learning a new language postpones the Alzheimer's decease by 4 years. There are also other skills that improve your cerebral capability like for example musical skills, especially learning to play a new musical instrument. In other words, learning skills can make you smarter.

Wide array of skills makes you also more appealing in the job market. Make sure to describe your skills on your CV in the most professional manner. It gets even better if you have certificates as the evidence of your skills.

If you are an employer, It's your responsibility to keep your workforces competent and skilled enough to perform the necessary tasks. Here's what Pallam Raju once said on the subject:

"Developing skills is as important as training. A larger effort is needed to create a skilled workforce with employment potential."

If you don't commit to this responsibility, it's going to be less probable that your company will achieve major success. Remember that even if the training expenses were high, the value you and your workforce get from learning new skills, is worth much more than the training expenses. You make a onetime payment for the training and in return you get something that you can use for the rest of your life for your benefit.

Don't focus on getting million dollars, but rather on serving million people

Do you ever think why you never made it big? Why you never reached success of your dreams? Maybe you got the whole concept wrong?

You see, many millionaires out there have been ambitious hard workers, who have sacrificed a lot in their lives to push them through to where they are now. Even though you might know all this, the fact that many of those who have earned at least one million dollars in total have really put their ego behind them and focused on how to serve people more efficiently.

If you are an entrepreneur, then you will need to do something for the other companies or other people. Everybody needs something and you need to be willing to be there to provide that something in best possible way within your power to achieve happy customers and continuous profit.

You don't need to be an Einstein to figure out how to sell people what they need. You don't need to be a genius to understand what skills you need to be a top athlete or a world class race driver. There's so many sources of information on the internet that you don't need to sweat about knowing the details once you figure out what you truly need.

But what is serving? For thousands of years people have served each other as servants or merchants for example. They have delivered other people what they need in a sufficient way. If they failed to deliver those things they way they were anticipated, they lost someone’s trust in them.

Take a look at the bigger picture here: Everybody around you and further away from you is a consumer. Consumers are those who consume something. There must be at least one product or one service you could come up with to make a lot of them happy or at least happier than before because you have something that they need and are willing to pay for.

But you might be asking: “How can I possibly have the time and resources to serve the million people all by myself?”. The answer is: You can’t do that all by yourself. That’s why you need to hire more people to help you serve those people and harvest the necessary resources while staying profitable.

Even at the times of economical depression you can find people to serve by being proactive. It’s how you reach them and what you offer them that counts.

Share your burden by hiring professionals

Whenever you feel that your own skills, strength or time aren't sufficient for contributing to your business activities, you should get someone to help you. There are always people to be found, who are willing to contribute their time and energy to help you, while receiving value for that. That value is most commonly money in forms of fixed or performance based salary; with or without commission or bonuses. Alternatively, especially if you are forming a start – up, you can offer your helpers some equity. You can give them some shares of your company. Should that be the case, they should have responsibility over some of the company's operations, depending on the size of the equity they receive. Their opinions will be heard at the meetings of the board of your company and this will motivate them to step up to the plate and push the envelope.

Great leadership qualities

Great leadership is not only showing your workforce how to do things, it's also the ability to genuinely ask for professional assistance and to generally inspire those who help you. By doing this, not only do you open doorways to others for them to endeavour on a new career opportunity, but you also increase the capacity of your company, lower your own efforts and keep your crew happy. By hiring someone you also show that you are a socially responsible businessman, who takes care of his community. This is often a valued feature that your local government can appreciate. As a reward you might get funding or tax breaks. You increase your chances for those rewards by supporting your local infrastructure.

After a while you might want to start selling the shares of your company. That's an easy way to make money. Make sure you keep your business running swell and reward your shareholders to keep them happy and buying even more of your shares.

Start-up

You have probably heard about Start-Ups. A start-up is a brand new company, formed by an individual or a group of people. In this case, having a group of people by your side to make new things happen saves you a lot of time and effort. That's because here you have people who are after the same things as you, success probably being on top of their list as well.

If you become the leader of your start up group, you will need to know how to manage and organize your people in order to achieve the best possible results. That has a critical impact on whether or not your company will start making big money. And the recipe for getting that big money is very simple: You don't spend a lot of money producing a gigantic amount of money at the same time. In order for you to be able to get that money from your company's account and transfer it to your account, you need to be clever. Make a deal with your workforce. Cap their annual income and uncap yours. Be the major shareholder and remain the owner, so that you will always have the control over the most of the capital that your company produces.

After all, your company is your empire. Within a certain set of rules, you can do anything to expand your empire and to expand your income.

Time distribution and timing

"Time that we have is the money that we don't have"

- Unknown

If the previous sentence seems unfamiliar to you then you must have heard this one: "Time is money". And it is true. Time might not equal money in the physical form, but it's a dimension which gives us the freedom to create something which in turn brings us money. In this chapter I'm going to tell you about how to use your time in the most profitable ways.

Time distribution

During the day our minds get usually occupied with various things. We spend time with other people face to face and online. The important thing for you is to assign as much time for the profitable activities as possible. Your days might be busy, or you might have many friends chatting with you on the instant messengers. Your days might slip without you making the right things to substantially develop new systems or implement them to create new streams of income or to enhance and scale up the existing ones.

Timing

First of all, what is timing? Timing is the capability to do something at a certain time. What you need to learn is to things the right time. Why? Because if you trade stocks or deal with real estate, you need to time your trades right in order to get the maximum profit. Do not undermine the importance of timing. At one moment it might be the right time to buy and at the other to sell.

Now let's examine the big picture of timing. Would you start selling protective amulets now? Of course not! People would think you're crazy, but before the end of 2012 people used to buy them like crazy. It was the end of an ancient Mayan calendar and those who knew what to sell right before the end of that year, earned big profit. So in this case timing is the ability to take advantage of the changing circumstances at the right time and earning money in the process.

Momentum

Momentum is another relevant word which you probably have heard before. No matter which word you use, the ability to make the right choices at the right time is priceless. It can lead you to great success and make you a lot of money. The key basketball players build momentum to score, the same applies for many other sports and also in business. You need to decide, when it the right time to make certain decisions for your benefit.

You can't build a factory before you have the finances and the city's approval for that, but you also don't need to wait with your thumbs crossed for that to happen. You just build momentum. You plan, you implement, you do everything that's necessary for that to happen. And when the time is right, you execute.

Develop customer oriented approach

In order to get value from your customers or clients, you need to develop a customer oriented approach, which will make your products and services more appealing to the buyer. Oftentimes potential customers abandon someone that provides great services or products just because they experienced horrible customer service. So you need to make sure that the person who brings the value to you gets quality treatment. That person doesn't necessarily even need to be a customer. It can also be partner or an employer. Your customer oriented approach will be working for your benefit and your value will rise in their eyes.

Treat your key network individuals as your best customers

If you were a customer how would you want to be treated? As you develop your network, you will eventually get a key network. So what is a key network? A key network is the individual or group of individual that will eventually take you far up the ladder. Very far. Those people you want to treat the best way possible. Even if some people treat you with ignorance and disrespect, you need to maintain professionalism.

If you are an employer, you need to make sure that your employees fully understand how important the customer oriented approach is. Make sure you oversee their interaction with the customers and try to get some feedback on the customer service quality from them. Your customer approach along with the quality of your product or service ultimately defines whether the customers are going to come back to spend their money or tell their friends, family and colleagues to do the same.

It pays to be polite

When you build your wealth, you need to be polite with the people who are involved in the process of making you money. That comprises your superiors, your clients, your customers, your fans, your subscribers and so on. It really pays to be polite. Nobody likes an ignorant or impolite individual. No matter how talented you are, if you insult someone and keep insulting them, you can probably say goodbye to your success, unless you are being paid for being a total jerk.

Finding a common ground

There is also something called finding a common ground, which allows you and your counterpart to find mutual interests without compromising your own. This applies especially in situations where you are about to make a deal with someone. There have been too many cases, where disputes have ended prominent attempts to create lucrative deals. So make sure you find that inner diplomat within you. A diplomat who can steer clear of pitfalls and will efficiently navigate his way to the treasure island and dig up the chest full of money.

No matter which field or industry you are trying to get rich in, politeness and diplomatic skills will always have high value. Those qualities need to be part of you, so that they represent you as well as your other competences. They also look good on your resume.

Beat your competitors

How competitive do you consider yourself? Do you like competing and winning or are you afraid to step up to the plate? You could compare the world of business to jungle, where only the strongest and smartest remain at the top of the food chain. When new leader candidates enter the herd, the tension rises because the leader of the herd might soon be swapped for another. Every single top dog wants to hold his position and is more or less afraid of losing it. The same thing applies to economical markets.

Let me say tell you the unpleasant news. Unfortunately the weakest people hardly ever reach major success. Being able to succeed in field with a lot of competition isn't easy by any means. There are tons of people like you and even better, who are willing to work more and get paid less for it. So in order to beat your competition you need to learn a couple of things.

Know your enemies

Your competition is your enemy, whether you wanted it or not. Like all the greatest warlords you need to learn how to beat your enemy. Examine the other businesses by forming a simple benchmarking strategy. Look for their weak spots. Find out what you can do better than them.

You can find real time information about your competitors in the newspaper publishings, online on their websites or by calling them or sending them an email enquiry. Of course nobody is going to give their corporate secrets on request, but by applying common sense and logic, you can soon find out what they are all about.

Competitive advantages

You should try beating your competitors with lower prices, better quality and more appealing customer service for example. The bottom line is that your competitive advantage needs to be something that you can beat your competitors with.

Jack Welch once remarked:

"If you don't have a competitive advantage, don't compete."

You get the picture now? Your success in a business environment that is filled with competition is a direct result of a distinct competition advantage. It's harder to up against a well established brand like Samsung for instance. The real challenge for starters and businesses that are in their growth stage is: how do they achieve that status of a well established business? You have to dig deep to find your competitive advantage that will keep your customers excited and always looking out for new products from you to spend their money on. If you are a talented musician. Your fans are your customers and you are the brand, while your recorded music is the product. Your unique style can be your very own competition advantage and you can remain the same or further develop it. Your actions affect the consumer trend.

Scale up your success

Don't comfort yourself with small achievements, they are just results of you contributing to your personal success. You know what many of the world class athletes were taught from the day one of their training? They were told to increase their efforts day after day one step at a time. Cumulative or in other words incrementing build up of your daily inputs is essential and completely realistic both in theory as in practise.

Threats of perfectionism

Don't always try to be perfect at something. It will only exhaust you both mentally and physically. However, if you are absolutely sure that perfectionism means no harm to you or your ability to make profit and keeps getting great results, then you should go for it. Do some testing before you know which path you take.

Your venture is you

You might have heard of the famous declaration Louis XIV, who stated that: "I am the state". Imagine yourself as a company. Whatever your trade is, you will definitely need to grow your business to get more money out of it. Your big success can be achieved gradually via small steps. Your grand wealth doesn't need to be formed overnight. Furthermore, getting rich overnight is extremely rare, unless you happen to win a lottery or receive a huge inheritance.

Take a minute to evaluate yourself as a company. Now start handling your business, like a successful company would do.

Anything can be scaled up

Scaling something up basically means adding more volume to something. You can scale up your success, your distress or your happiness. You don't need to keep everything level. Scaling up isn't always as difficult as many think. It's a coordinated pattern of actions that's often been pre-planned before it ever takes place.

Let's bring an example. We could be talking about scaling up production at a local factory. The production needs to be scaled up due to increased demand in your product. So what do you do? Well first you make sure you have enough resources for expanding your supply. By resources I mean capital, in other words money. The next step is to increase the supply of raw materials to your factory according to the demand you are facing, caused by your customers. Then, you need to make sure that you have enough space in your factory for additional crew. You will need to hire more workers. Make sure that supervision of those workers will be sufficient and the safety standards are met. Then just enjoy your additional income!

That's a basic example of how you scale up your production.

Ensure your legal protection: patents, copyrights and agreements

As someone aiming for the financial stratosphere, it's essential to know what measures need to be taken to make sure that nobody is taking advantage of you, without paying the price. Agreements, contracts and copyrights should be on one of your priorities if you are starting something massive that's going to bring you huge amounts of money.

Copyright

If you decide to write a book, you need to be mindful of getting a copyright agreement. Nothing obliges you to get one, but if you don't, there's a good chance that someone might steal the plot of your book. In court, you don't stand a chance if your material isn't legally protected.

Patent

if you happen to invent something, do not let anyone steal the idea behind your invention. Have it patented. Getting your invention patented is a pretty straightforward process. After you have created and tested your prototype and you have your technical documentation clearly describing your innovation, you should visit your local patenting office and fill up their patenting form, make a payment and deliver every piece of documentation that they require and then just wait for the patent to come through. In some cases, the prototype isn't obligatory requirement for a patent. You can just patent the idea.

Agreement

Always try to get a good agreement from a lawyer, if you can afford it . However, if you can't afford it, let someone else help you or do it by yourself. There are plenty of free downloadable agreement templates on the internet. Make sure it's as detailed and foolproof as possible with regard to defending your rights.

Disclaimer

Often those who haven't made any agreements or even disclaimers, have ran into problems and sometimes had to declare a bankruptcy when another party wronged them and got away with it. You should act smarter. Make a foolproof disclaimer, stating the terms of service and put it on your company website. Ask all your clients to read and accept the terms of service prior to purchasing your product or service. If someone breaches those terms, you will have enough evidence against them in court. This evidence you can find in your email folder if the order was made electronically. If majority of your orders are made through telephones, just record your business calls.

Every piece of legal protection isn't only saving you from potentially encountering huge losses along the way, but it's also giving your company a lot of credibility and adding more value to your brand.

Make use of your true talent

All of us are gifted with something that we have had from our very birth. In other words, we all have talents. Some of us are great writers, some can sing or paint pictures. Some people are intellectually more gifted than the others and this brings them great results in fields like mathematics or physics.

You and I have talents as well. Whatever it is you're good at and you enjoy doing. You might even call it as your hobby. Did you know that you could actually make money out of your hobbies? This way you could devote your time to something that you really enjoy and which brings you wealth in the same time. A lot of people have turned their hobby into a million dollar income. Just look at the most famous professional athletes for instance. They make millions just for doing what they love, so I bet they're having a lot of fun earning their money too.

Arthur Schopenhauer once said:

"Talents hits a target no one else can hit"

Your talent basically allows you to reach higher heights and achieve something that a regular person is just incapable of achieving. You could be super flexible acrobat, highly skilled magician, an opera singer with simply magnificent voice or your music band could be the best in its genre.

You probably have one or two talents that you may or may not have noticed already. So do some thinking in order to find out, whether you could monetize on your talents. It might actually turn out to be your thing. Something that you were meant to do for a living.

Sometimes there are those who do want to gain profit from exercising their talent, but they just don't know how to do it. Well it's not that hard really. You just need to *demonstrate* your talent so that nobody will doubt that you are good at what you do. If you speak 25 different languages, make a YouTube video of you practicing those languages and add the link of your video to your resume. Your recruiters will surely be positively dazzled.

If you really want to build a fortune by using your talents, build a company or sign a very lucrative deal. Don't just sit around and waiting for people to start throwing money at you. You need to act now and start building your reputation. Always remember that people usually tend to be looking out for their own interests, so don't expect your path to success be all bright and rosy. It's probably going to be many things which you didn't expect: Scary, exhausting and challenging. On the other hand it can be extremely exciting. It can turn out to be the best time of your life. The question is: What do you have to lose? Are you willing to sacrifice the things that block your way to success? Are you willing to fight for your fortune? If yes, then get out there and do it!

Become a great negotiator

Let every eye negotiate for itself and trust no agent.

- *William Shakespeare*

If you can form a great relationship, you should already have some basics of a good negotiator. There are many things in life which are negotiable, like your salary, prices of goods and terms of a contract. Negotiating basically means two or more opponents with different interests crafting beneficial results for themselves. It's the art of making deals, something that can really differentiate a true businessman from the others.

Unless if you are a natural negotiator, the more you practice negotiating, the better your skills grow. The more deals you negotiate, the more likely it is that you will reach a successful deal that will bring you one step closer to having at least million dollars on your bank account.

The art of negotiation

Negotiating is really quite simple. Let's start from the basics. Like in all the proper houses, you need a foundation. You need to have proper diplomatic skills and politeness in your tone. Don't forget to smile and greet at the start of negotiation. You need to create a friendly atmosphere and your words must be clear and nonthreatening. It might be a good idea to joke or say something funny just to break the ice. You will need to create an atmosphere that makes others relaxed.

Choosing the right strategy

Different strategies apply to different people. Your main purpose is to reach your goal by negotiating the terms that are most favourable to you. This might take a lot of convincing, but by using a comprehensible approach, you can reach your target quite soon. Sometimes it's good to let your opponent speak and let him think that he's in control. Sometimes you need to feed information to someone like a programmer in order to achieve the desired result.

Exercising your negotiation skills

Sometimes it's good to bargain about things that seem insignificant. For example, if you are having a vacation in a third world country and find yourself on a market filled with bunch of cheap stuff, you should try to bargain just for the sake of exercise. In some countries negotiators are highly welcomed to those marketplaces. In other countries, however, bargaining can be seen as a rude habit, so make sure you find out about the local impacts of that particular practice before you fully engage in it.

You can always choose an opponent amongst the people you already know and engage in a friendly negotiation contest with him just to sharpen your skills. Both of you have a different agenda and both of you have price caps and minimums which you need to keep. The winner is the one who has reached the most favourable deal.

Learn to sell anything

Life is full of selling. Whether it's asking someone to buy your product, persuading someone to join your team or making your audience adore you, you need to know how to sell.

You can't avoid selling on your way to success. A talented singer might not give a sales pitch, but will perform convincingly enough to get all the talent scouts interested. That's selling. Later on the manager of the singer needs to *sell the performer* to different people in order get some money out of it. Or imagine yourself sitting in front of a recruiter at a job interview. What are you doing? That's right: selling.

The basics of selling

Often salesmen make a grave mistake by approaching their customer in a wrong way. They start telling about their product or service or whatever it is that their selling. It's wrong because the customer will most likely react in a negative way. Let's me explain this with an example.

Salesman: Hello! My name is (blah blah), I'm from the (blah, blah). Do you have a moment?
Customer: Umm... Yea, why not....
Salesman: Excellent! We have just launched a new product its very ....(blah, blah, blah) I think you really should buy it!
Customer: Hmm... I don't know, I really must ask someone first (I don't trust you). I'll think about it (you will never hear from me again!).

Does this sound familiar? No matter which situation you are in, no matter what you are selling, just confronting people in a dull way just doesn't work! You need to create demand *in* your customer. The customer might not know that he needs something and you need let the customer know that whatever you are selling is something that the customer simply can't live without.

Recipe of selling anything to anyone

Whether your customer is your spouse, your business partner or even your child, in order for you to be able to sell your agenda, you need to approach them by offering them direct value, asking your customer questions about what they want and what they need. A great salesperson can always provide what customer truly needs. You need to be enthusiastic. You need to excited when selling something like it's the best thing that happened to you. provide enough valuable information and some details explaining why your product it superior to your competitor's products. Your salesman skills correlate to your overall success. A great salesman always sees even the smallest hints of opportunity and leverages them effectively without hesitation. Always believe in what you are selling. Just follow Nick Woodman's advice:

"I can sell anything that I totally believe in, but I'm a horrible salesman of something I don't believe in."

CHAPTER 3

A Few Concrete Ways Of Making Millions

Here are just a few basic examples of ways people have become millionaires with a brief, but

overall fundamental description of how they did it.

Multitasking 101

One of the greatest multitaskers in history, was Julius Caesar. He could do several different things at once.

But what actually is multitasking? Multitasking is the ability to be immersed in many processes at the same time. This doesn't actually mean that you would have to talk on the phones to several people at once while typing on the keyboard by using your left foot drinking coffee by using your right foot.

I'm talking about multitasking, where you are responsible of several different projects on many different levels. There are some risks with multitasking though. It is very natural for people to be concentrated on one task or project at a time while neglecting the other ones in terms of quality. I know what I'm talking about. When I was just starting to multitask seriously I ran into that particular problem. What you need to do, is use a special approach to tackle this issue.

Channel your attention

In order to be successful at several processes at once, you need to be able to channel your attention to the right direction at the right time.

If you coordinate all of your projects remotely via computer, you need to learn to type fast.

Freelance multitasking by telecommuting

This is actually the cherry on the top of the cake. This is how you actually get rich. Freelance multitasking and part time multitasking does not oblige you to commit to your work the same way as a full time office job for example. Freelance workers are those who work on separate projects often as the contractors, although freelancers have usually much more freedom on their hands. And contractors often get paid much better than full time workers. Telecommuting is remote working. It's working from your home office or a hammock on a Caribbean island. And here's the good news: There are no restrictions on how many different projects you can work on at the same time. You can have one or you can have ten of them!

If your freelance projects result in steady profit with some recurring income then you are walking on the path to becoming a millionaire. Your next step is scaling things up. If you think that you've taken too many projects, more than you can chew, then you could easily outsource them to third party members from websites like Elance.com or Freelancer.com. Make sure that you have a clear profit margin and that your freelancer is delivering great results on time.

If you absolutely love working on several processes at once, then multitasking is your cup of tee. I know exactly how great multitasking can feel. I've done it and I intend to continue doing it.

Marry a multimillionaire

Marrying a millionaire or a billionaire is a fast track to potentially becoming a millionaire. Your new spouse could share his/her wealth with you. Keep in mind however that this does not guarantee that you will be a millionaire, but you will probably be living like one. Imagine all the fast cars, private jets, boats and limo rides that would be at your disposal, not to mention living at a luxury home?

There are, however, some difficulties regarding this option. Not everyone is capable of marrying a rich person not to mention the fact that you might not even be even willing to do so. It's more of a clique that gives easy access mostly to young and beautiful women to enjoy the lifestyle that they always dreamed of. There are many housewives that are just sitting home and enjoying the good life while their husbands are out on a business making millions. From a moral point of view, often a question or two arises: How fair is that? Those who have worked for years to achieve their millions often generously share their wealth with you if they truly love you, but you better not cross or displease them because you might be kicked out even before you know it.

There's no reason why young men couldn't become husbands for elderly millionaire women. In fact that's not unusual case scenario either. One might bring up a topic of gold digging here, but if true love is involved then hey, what's the big deal?

Often rich spouses give their new "love acquisitions" an exceptional chance to thrive and become successful themselves. They introduce them with the right people or give them sufficient starting capital to build their own company and provide them with the guidance of the best consultants in the field. That's just a possible scenario. There can be many other scenarios as well that can further enhance your possibilities to work your way to the playground of the top financial sharks.

There are also those who make their money divorcing a millionaire. The strategy is simple: Seduce, get married and get a divorce. Without a prenuptial agreement, a divorce might grant you half of the fortune. Usually the millionaires are smart enough to smell the gold diggers though.

Nevertheless if you have a solid relationship with someone who's worth millions, then you shouldn't worry much. Money usually clears a lot of problems and there's no resource that can help you make money more efficiently than money. So follow the money and you will find your success.

Get lucky at a game of chance

Games of chance are very popular because they often have very high jackpots. Often the grand winner of a lottery game, for instance, wins a money prize that is worth several millions of dollars. And just to think of it: It's not that difficult really. All you need to do is buy the lottery ticket and collect the winning amount, piece of cake! At least that's how we would like to imagine it.

Winning against the odds

It's not that simple in real life. The odds of you winning millions of dollars from a lottery game or any other game of chance are very much against you. It's highly unlikely that you will ever win a million dollar prize in a game of chance, but there's been many people that have historically beaten the odds. If you consider yourself one of those lucky people then go ahead and try a game of luck by all means, but be aware that nothing guarantees that you will win anything. You might be even better off selling lottery tickets or sweepstakes yourself and becoming a millionaire that way.

If you're serious about diving into the games of chance, the first thing you should do, is to look for a game that has the best odds for you to win and the best payouts. You might consider betting on a racetrack, but make sure that you research everything there is to know about those races and particularly the horses.¨

Logic of it

Betting is really easy, it's just you don't get to win that much unless you are betting in a fixed game and those ones are very rare and most likely not even legal. Still, some of us find themselves being favoured by lady luck and receive a large winning amounts to their accounts just for betting on some random numbers. Some people say that there are special lucky numbers that seem to be producing more wins than the other numbers. Actually that statement has no mathematical logic to it, since the winning numbers are nowadays most commonly generated by random number generator.

There have been cases when hackers have tried to program the so called slots to give maximum profit instantly. These days it's very improbable that someone could be able to pull a stunt like that and get away with it successfully, thanks to the powerful surveillance technology in casinos where one can commonly find these machines that are filled with coins.

Lucky strike in Vegas

Speaking of machines filled with coins, one can find those most commonly in cities like Las Vegas or Atlantic City. However, there are casinos and casino resorts all around the planet, but some countries don't actually allow gambling within their borders. So just imagine that you're on one of your holiday trips to Vegas and you hit a slot machine and drop a coin there and suddenly you win the jackpot! Now what would be a more thrilling way to instantly become a millionaire? A word of warning though: Don't get too excited chasing the jackpot. You might actually lose a lot of money without winning any decent amounts of money in the process.

But it is more common for those who play more often to win more often and it makes perfect sense.
So if you play occasionally and bet every now and then, you might eventually hit that mega jackpot.

Become a professional gambler

Have you ever thought, what would it be like to spend your days in casinos? Even though a great deal of casino gambling winnings are acquired by pure luck, there are still games where player can actually cut down some of the house edge by applying skills. The player can also improve his odds by applying different strategies. One of the games, where strategy comes in handy is Blackjack. If you apply the optimal strategy perfectly, you are looking at a very low house edge, which makes winning more probable.

However, if you don't want to compete against the house edge, you should pick poker as your game. There are several poker professionals, who have started with very tiny playing funds and made millions during their poker careers. If you want to start a career of a gambler, you need to be aware of some basic things.

Firstly, you can't expect to win every time. You have to count on your betting and bluffing skills. In order to enhance both of them, you need to practise. Find out more information about your game and learn new tactics that you can use at the gambling tables. While you are playing, you should keep track of your gambling budget. Most professional gamblers can't afford to live lavishly. On average they make a few hundred dollars a day because conservative betting is the safest way to ensure their income in the field of professional gambling. However, if you manage to get to the top and become the best of the best, then you could very well be looking at millions of dollars in your gambling revenue. Many high level poker professionals join the poker tournaments to battle at the final table for high stakes. Those tournaments usually last several days, but the main prizes are huge.

Strategy is your best bet

When you are starting out, you should keep in mind that the strategy is your best bet. Don't go by your gut instinct unless you are incredibly lucky. Speaking of luck, some people believe that they are luckier than others by definition. Actually luck isn't something that can be quantifiably measured. If there is some sort of probability for some event to occur, it may certainly occur, but if the probability is not 100% and someone just keeps winning, it means that the player is cheating.

Cheating while gambling isn't something you want to take a chance with. However, if you decide to cheat, you have extremely low chances to be successful. The casino security can easily spot cheaters, who might face thousands of dollars in fines or even imprisonment.

The business gamble

Casinos are designed to profit from players, so if you are a businessman, you could think of flipping the whole picture around. Why not become a casino owner? The casinos don't provide guaranteed income, but there are still fairly good odds for that gamble to be profitable for you.

If casinos aren't your cup of tea, you could still get entertained by casual gaming and inspired by reading about the latest events in the industry. The biggest casinos generate unbelievable amounts of profit and becoming familiar with their brands and marketing methods can give you the idea of how a successful business really promotes its image.

Or then again, you could just go sit at a poker table and beat everyone, get addicted to the game and start winning millions of dollars. It's up to you to decide, which door of opportunities you will choose.

Become a sports professional

There are plenty of sports that have resulted in financially lucrative careers. Just look at Tiger Woods, Michael Jordan or any other sports icon that is often mentioned in the sports section of your local newspaper. Even though they play in different categories of sports, there's one thing that they mostly have in common. They've all made millions of dollars.

The way of a sports millionaire

If you feel that you are particularly good at golf for example, why not take your game to the next level? Practise your skills and participate at a small competition. If you prove to be successful, advance gradually to the bigger competitions until you become the world champion. That's how many sports millionaires have made their way to the top of their career and earned their riches.

There is a downside to this path, however. If you're not particularly good at some highly popular sport, like golf or tennis, then you're probably never going to earn that big money. And where does that big money come from? Well lets trace it. Winning competitions and championships brings money, but not only that. If you are extremely good at the mainstream sports, you can cut yourself a sponsorship deal which will keep bringing you money as long as you wear their sportswear with their logo being easily recognized. You can also make a ton of money by being an advertising model for wristwatch companies or fragrance companies. Attend talk shows and get movie roles... the list goes on and on. If you are the number one sports professional in your field even for a short while, then you will become famous and fame will sell you with ease, as you probably already know.

Notice how the sports legends just keep coming back? Maybe they are doing something that they love or maybe they are doing it because that's when the money comes in faster than ever.

Even if you aren't very young anymore, you could still thrive in sports like ping pong for example. If you can beat anyone at chess, start winning competitions and gradually move to larger contests. That's how world champions make their way to the top.

If you are not a sporty type, you can try and become a manager of a football team for instance. You would be responsible of trading the players. That means buying and selling them. It sounds a bit harsh, but that's just part of the business in professional sports. You could make plenty of money while crafting the best sports team ever.

Sports is just another path where you can reach extraordinary levels of success if you are exceptionally good at what you are doing, but if you also enjoy what you are doing, your chances of becoming successful improve drastically and the level of the success you can achieve increases.

Hunt for the hidden riches

Treasure hunting might sound like a children's game, but the truth is that many hidden treasures are worth millions of dollars. Those hidden treasures might be represented in ancient coins, jewellery or artefacts. There are many treasure hunters out there that run their own operations on sea and on land. The sea exploration requires financial resources and equipment. Museums love to have new shiny artefacts in their collections and many private collectors are willing to pay incredible amounts just to buy your newfound ancient object and add it to their collection.

Sometimes people have found old artefacts while digging in close premises, sometimes as close as their own backyard! However don't go digging holes in your backyard if you suddenly get the gold rush. At least not without using a metal detector first.

Also, hunting for precious metals like gold and silver can really prove to be worth your while. Actually gold, silver and oil are the real natural treasures and by discovering them and claiming ownership over them will definitely skyrocket your wealth.

The arctic playground

Even though everybody seems to be talking about peak oil being reached, it doesn't overrule the fact that oil could still make you rich. If you happened to discover a large reserve of crude oil somewhere and manage to get the ownership of that oil, that would be an instant jackpot for you. This is one of the reasons why so many Nordic countries are so interested in obtaining their piece of the arctic "playground". The melting ice is revealing large pockets of oil on the bottom of the ocean. It takes vessels, such as ice breakers and experts, like petroleum geologists and commercial divers along with saturation divers and engineers to be able to play the critical part in locating and retrieving the valuable "black gold".

To infinity and beyond

There are still many unknown secrets in the world that lie hidden awaiting for those who dare and are cleaver enough to discover them, but what about the materials that can be found in space, on asteroids and on other planets? As the space flight technology keeps developing, it is said that the geological explorations might expand beyond our earthly premises. Imagine hundreds of robots drilling valuable materials on the objects that are orbiting somewhere in reachable distances? You could be the future billionaire if you find a way how to harness the technology and organize the drilling operations in space.

Even if you weren't after the precious metals or minerals, you could still make money on ever so mysterious space. Just look at what Richard Branson and Elon Musk have achieved. Space flights will probably be more mainstream in the near future than ever before. At least that's what some scientists are predicting. Thanks to the developing space flight technology, the space flights might actually be much more affordable within in the next decades. So why not offer affordable weekend trips to space or discovery explorations to nearby planets? Even if the technology isn't here yet, you could already start planning your foothold in this industry and gain enormous advantage when the time comes.

You don't need to be extremely intellectual or very well connected to pull this off. So many people with the same brains as you and me have used the information available, brought people together and started to work towards completion of a common vision. You will need a lot of persistence and you should have the necessary knowledge and resources for the sake of your own credibility and success of your venture.

Write and publish a book

Many people have become rich by publishing their own book. If you enjoy writing then this is definitely something you should consider doing.

Picking the genre

Choosing the genre can be a challenge if you're not sure on which topic you are going to write your book. You can write a simple "How To..." eBook for example, which instructs your readers on how to do something. However, you should know that a lot of this kind of information can already be found on the internet for free so in this case the demand can become a problem. I recommend to think seriously about whether you are going to write a historical novel or a Ski-Fi – story for example. Writing an entire book is a project that takes time and persistence.

The expenses

In the book writing business the expenses would mainly comprise the publishing and marketing costs. You will probably need to hire a graphic designer to design a front page cover for your book, unless you can handle it yourself.

Writing a book can be a profitable venture, but nothing guarantees that you will earn a living by writing unless you can make a name for yourself by being very talented and finding a good niche while choosing your topic. If you can write an interesting fictional story that becomes as successful as J.K. Rowling's or Dan Brown's books, then all you have to do is write the sequels to that book. Productising is not that hard: Find a publishing company and a distributor and start marketing.

Writing requires a lot of time and dedication. At times it can be frustrating and if you get emotional about your writing project and its ups and downs it can really eat you up. If you can create fantastic stories, entertain and inspire people, then they might actually willingly come back for more of your production. Now that's where it gets tricky. So how do you target large masses of people? How will you seduce them all?

Addressing large masses of people

Success at writing publications lies in being able to make a lot of people buy your book. So you need to address the major segments or people from different groups, taking into account their age, gender, race and other characteristics. In this case you wouldn't be writing to just a tiny fragmental target group, but a large segment, which has universal features inside of it.

Following that path, eventually those who read that book will give great feedback to it, critics among others will boost yours sales through great reviews. "New York Times Best Seller" on the front page of your book can further crank up your sales. So make sure you write good stuff that a lot of people can relate to and be entertained by.

The worst case scenario, on the other hand is, that your reputation as a writer gets totally destroyed and nobody will buy your books ever again.

Become a Hollywood actor

The world is a stage and we are all merely players

- William Shakespeare

You probably have wondered at least once in your life, what would it be like to become a Hollywood actor? A lot of people have asked themselves the same question. There are many different actors in Hollywood, but most of the biggest names out there have something in common. They get millions of dollars for what they do.

Becoming a high paid Hollywood actor is by no means an easy task. It's a tough industry to get in and to be successful at, but it's also one of the most exciting ones as well. First thing you need to do is you need to get some acting experience. Enrol for acting classes at a local theatre or apply for a job as a member of the filming staff. You could even volunteer as an unpaid member of the crew. As a result you would get a lot of valuable experience.

First you need to create a resume. You should go to a professional photographer and take a few headshots for your application. Also, you should create an application video, where you introduce yourself and improvise for a few minutes. A video that lasts 1 minute is way too short and the one that goes on and on after 10 minute mark is going to be too long. As a thumb rule 5 minute long videos usually work the best.

Your next step is to search for auditions. By this time, you should have your presentation and communication skills sharpened up and your stress endurance skills high enough, so that you wouldn't faint or embarrass yourself in front of people who might hire you for the role.

The acting itself requires you to memorize your lines, to invoke emotions by your performance and to improvise. Camera shyness won't lead you to success in this industry.

Becoming rich and successful in Hollywood carries something that some might consider a burden. In other words fame. Can you handle being super famous? While a lot of people do enjoy fans screaming for their autographs, they might not be too overjoyed about paparazzis harassing you at every corner. And what about the gossips tabloids will spread about you? Could you handle that too? If so then you are on the path, which might be the most exciting time of your life someday, but if you can't handle those things, it might lead to severe alcohol or drug problems. This path of tragedies might even lead to your early grave, so you better think twice on this one.

Bear in mind that the life of an actor might not be as flashy as you might think it is. It's actually hard work and those who do it simply because they love acting and not for the money often get to the top where they make more money. On the other hand, as ironical as it might sound, those who do it just for the money and fame, often don't become very successful.

Make fortune in the real estate market

Real estate business has been the major money maker for those who have managed to play smart enough in the Real Estate field.

Lucrative brokerage

There are many types of Real Estate roles you can pursue. If you have great interpersonal and extraordinary selling skills, you could become a real estate broker. Real estate companies are mostly paying their brokers only a commission from every deal the broker makes. The best brokers out there make seven figures a year.

But why being a broker, if you can have others working for you? Owning a real estate company is a great because you pay your brokers only for the sold real estate, while you focus on marketing and scaling up your real estate empire.

The path of a real estate developer

If none of these two options suit you, then you should consider the role of a real estate developer. The idea behind real estate developing is really straightforward. You just buy a cheap property, which requires refurbishment. You remodel the house thus raising its market value and sell it for a higher price. Alternatively, if it's a large complex which comprises several flats, you could rent it out and get recurring profit that way.

Speaking of recurring profit, investing in real estate is probably the most common way of making money on real estate these days. All you need to do is buy a property and rent it out. Your long term profit expectancy is stable, but usually it takes years for your property to pay itself out.

Find a hot real estate market

Whatever your choice is, you should know that the real estate market often reflects the local economy, so it might be your best bet to relocate someplace, where the real estate market is hot. You should pick a location, where there's a high demand for real estate property. Higher demand makes the prices go up and if you take advantage of that, a big slice of that money may end up in your pocket.

If you suddenly notice that some particular area is being developed. It might be a great idea to buy a property nearby. Sooner or later a real estate tycoon might offer to buy it from you for much more than it's actually worth. So that's one way to make quick and easy profit.

Make sure you plan ahead to cover all the angles before you start putting money into something in order to make money. Make sure that you are absolutely on top of what's going on and what's going to happen. There are always risks involved and you won't make a very good businessman if you aren't able to calculate those risks. After you've covered all the angles and finished planning, it's time to execute your plan and do the best to get that huge profit coming to your bank account that you've always dreamt of.

Invent something new

While inventing itself may be seem as something that is associated with the smartest and the most gifted of us, inventing is actually something that is within reach of virtually anyone's capabilities. Any new physical device can be patented. Bear in mind though that a new patented device will not make you rich unless there will be demand for it and you have the resources to turn it into the hottest product on the market.

Inventing something new is a process that can take a lot of time. While the idea of a new invention might occur to you instantly, there are many other stages to it as well. You will need to plan all the steps of designing and manufacturing your invention into physical form, making it consumer friendly and ultimately turning it into a product, ready for mass production.

Your invention does not need to be a piece of cutting edge technology, although you innovating something new in that field certainly wouldn't hurt you at all. After all, technology is rapidly being developed basically in most of the fields of our everyday life. Sometimes there are special sponsor programs for those who manage to create software or technology for specific purposes that have already been designated. If you are that curious inventor type, who can create most extraordinary things, then you should definitely go for it. Many inventors have traded their old bikes for luxury cars upon successfully productizing their useful invention.

Inventing something useful

Your invention must be useful and needed for the vast population if you are planning to make money out of it. It can be anything new whatsoever that individual consumers or companies would willing to spend their money on. Later on you will need to patent your invention and possibly start producing massive copies of the invention of yours. Imagine how proud it can make you feel to see thousands if not millions of people using your own invention! If your invention has true demand and you have managed to patent it successfully, productizing your product is going to be relatively straightforward. If you're not into setting up your own production, just make deal with other companies that will willingly do that for you. The licensing deals and royalties will keep the money coming in your pocket even if you don't set up your own production line.

What you need is a curious and progressive mindset. You're not going too far by thinking "everything that's worth inventing, has already been invented". There's still plenty of room or empty void for new scientific discoveries and new innovations. Speaking of scientific discoveries, it's often a good idea to team up with some very efficient scientists before you go for the deep unknown. It's usually much harder to accomplish anything great all by yourself, but if you are, a creative genius, who absolutely needs peace and solitary harmony in order to create something brand new, you shouldn't fight your true nature. After all, sometimes serenity is required to reach some stages of inner concentration that is required to make all kinds of breakthroughs.

If you ever face lack of inspiration you could look back at the great inventors such as Archimedes, Leonardo Da Vinci and Thomas Edison. Read their biographies and just be amazed at what great achievements can come out of those genius and persistent minds. You and me are the same species, same flesh and blood as those great inventors. It means that we can do anything if we try hard enough!

Use social media to get rich

Do you know how many simple ways there are that make millions? You wouldn't believe if I told you! If you love blogging, choose a blogging platform and start creating those great blogs.

Million dollar blogger

What is considered a past time activity or just a hobby, can make you millions. Blogging is actually very easy. All you need to do for starters is to find a topic that interests you the most and start writing some text. Even half a page of text is enough.

There are many great blogging platforms out there, such as WordPress or Blogger. By applying some basic search engine optimization, you could get visibility for your blog and get more clicks, in other words more viewers who leave comments on your blog. This is one way of how you can achieve more visibility and of course popularity on the internet. And if business see that you are popular, they might offer you deals worth of tens of thousands of dollars if not more just for letting you market their product on your site.

YouTube millionaire

Other than blogging, you can use YouTube to make yourself rich. The trick is to get enough viewers and make deals with affiliates and promoters. Post their ad under your vid (video) or add it to the vid itself if it's a commercial and voila! Soon you will be getting commission from buyers of the products you just promoted. It might sound simple, but getting millions of viewers is not that easy as it seems. Once again you need to find a niche that hasn't been used that much, but can generate high popularity. Ever heard of videos that have gone viral? It means videos that have spread exponentially on the internet, like a virus, cramping up the viewer ratings like crazy. That's what you should aim for and if you do it correctly, you will have several promoters and affiliates offering you deals. When that happens, just choose the highest bidder and start making profit. You shouldn't promote too many affiliates in one vid because that's going to hurt your "YouTube channel brand" in the long run. If you are new to making YouTube vids, find some tutorials on the internet and just practise until you get it.

Facebook monetizing

If Facebook is an environment you truly enjoy, if it's a place where you truly feel creative, then you could try making money on Facebook. Millions of people spend hours on Facebook every day, updating their own profiles and checking status updates of other people. Facebook is a wonderful marketplace, where you could advertise virtually anything.

Make money by playing online RPG's

The traditional role playing board games like Dungeons and Dragons have evolved after the beginning of the internet age, becoming an arena, crowded with millions of players who often spend real money to buy some in-game products, like armour, gear or other kind of virtual equipment. It goes without saying that in order to make some serious money while playing online RPG's, you should be well established in your virtual environment. You should be high levelled and famous having reached substantial popularity and thus developed your own virtual brand out of your virtual character and possibly even guild that you belong to. The key is to merchandize all the tradable in-game stuff for the real money.

Become an affiliate marketing wiz

If writing isn't your thing, then you should try something that has been tried out for decades on the internet. Something that has brought great results such as millions of dollars! I'm talking about something that started to gain huge popularity not so long ago. Affiliate marketing! The affiliate marketing could be your moneymaking machine, if you know how to do it right.

Affiliate marketing means basically working as an affiliate of a vendor, who has a product or service and needs other people to market their goods. In return for marketing for your vendor, you get a percentage of the sales for every product that is sold through your advert. This can be done by posting a link to various places on the internet or creating a clickable banner that works the same way as the previously mentioned link.

Affiliate marketing isn't an easy field to get profit these days. Many think that the golden age of affiliate marketing was in the late 90's and early 2000's. These days, when marketing seems to be ambivalent in the internet, everyone seems to be having an integrated marketing filter in their minds. We might not even realize it, but we do feel irritated of those marketing ads and our first reaction to seeing one is usually moving on. It is said that the average time for an average person to look at an ad is about 4 seconds. In 4 seconds that person will form a decision whether he is interested in the message that's being advertised or not. So you as an affiliate you need to empress the internet surfers immediately.

Differentiate yourself from the flock and make it staggering by its appearance and its content.

The other thing you can do, is you can recruit other people to do the marketing for you. You can promise them a certain share of your cut and they will do the job for you. Many people on the internet would like to get some extra money. If you explain them exactly what it is they need to do and pay them a cut of your share, you could easily increase your revenue. it's better let the others do the work for you, but make sure that you teach them all about it first. The best case scenario is that you'll be looking at great recurring income. Recurring income can be achieved by selling something that regular membership payments for example.

To get into the affiliate marketing, you will need to search for the sites that offer affiliate marketing for newcomers. There are sites where you can set up an affiliate account, where you'll be paid. On the same site there's often also a marketplace, where you can find the products that are sold by online vendors. Those products should have affiliate marketing links attached to them. If you have set up your account, then those links should be automatically associated with your account. In other words when you paste that link somewhere on the internet and someone clicks on it and buys the product, the commission will automatically go to your account without any extra steps for you to take. It's a relatively straightforward way to make money, but it can take a lot of effort and some skills to make your marketing content appealing enough.

There are many discussion boards or web forums for marketing professionals, where you can read some valuable advices. There you can also get in touch with successful marketing professionals.

Develop your career - work for a high salary

Working for high salary is something that most people consider as the only they could ever become rich. “Get a degree and get a high paying job!”, said your mommy and daddy.

Working for the man

You can indeed become a millionaire if you work as a doctor at a private clinic somewhere in the USA for example, but do you really have what it takes to become one? And is it worth your while to spend all those years and the tuition money trying to become one? You've got to love treating patients and you've got to be ok with cutting corpses...At some point. Oh yeah, and when the pandemic hits your town, you'll be on the front line intercepting its first victims.

Okay, maybe becoming a doctor isn't your thing. How about becoming a stock broker? You could get rich, but do you have the necessary sales skills and stamina to work your way to becoming a millionaire at that trade? Most of us like to picture our future bright as a clear sky on a sunny day. Many of us think that future will bring a high paying job. No. It doesn't work that way. Time to wake up. The future isn't your genie in the bottle and there is no such thing as a free mail order success. If you want to become rich by becoming an employee, you better have the right qualification, references and some good contacts to pull a few strings. You also need to learn how to set your ego aside.

Ruthless 9 to 5 schedule

Alarm clock rings. Wake up. Brush your teeth. Dress up. Drink your coffee. Drive to work. Work like a dog. Drive back. Go to sleep.... That's what we call a regular working day. I might have missed a few details here and there and the content of working day depends by the individual , but that is not the point. The point is do you like to live like this? If you work at your cubicle for a small salary, would you be able to be the one who strives for perfection, promotion and eventually acquiring a managerial position? Managers often get six figure income and a million dollar capital is just a matter of time for them. Here's an honest question for you: Do you enjoy your rat race? You're better enjoy it because bitter and gloomy workers will hardly ever skyrocket their careers if they keep being constantly displeased and choose to educate everyone about their misery.

The higher you climb on your career ladder, the higher responsibilities you will get. If you can handle them and prove everyone that you are up for it, then career developing could be something you should seriously consider. Eventually, if you manage to rise to a key position within a large organization, you might be very well given some company stocks, options and bonuses which will then add up to your total income.

It really pays to be a CEO

Well the headline says it all. It pays to be a CEO, it really does. The salary structure of CEO's, who are leading major companies, has skyrocketed within the last few years. Those CEO's can really expect to be making millions. Wouldn't that make a great career achievement?

Become a public speaker

Did you know that the world's best public speakers get paid millions of dollars for just speaking to the audience for a few hours? Wouldn't that be a great way to become mega rich? Then keep on reading.

Million dollar speech

Don't get too excited yet: Before you can even consider having your own audience, you first need to master the topic that you want to specialize in. You need to have passion for the topic so that you could really earn your money. You need to be a great stage speaker too. If your audience likes you, they might even recommend you to everyone they know and probably come back on another occasion.

Your topic could be something like: "How to get more customers" or "How to be more confident in life". Here we have two different types of public speaking, the latter of which is defined as motivational speaking.

Motivational speaking

If you've seen Tony Robbins or other motivational speakers on stage, then you know the basics of what it's all about. If you are willing to take on the path of a motivational speaker, you need to be comfortable standing on a stage and talking in front of a lot of different people. And you will not be just talking, but you will be *motivating* them. As a motivator you would be required to show leadership qualities in a sense of leading the people to the new kind of lifestyle, a lifestyle full of motivation.

In order to be a good motivational speaker, it's necessary to get influenced by the leading motivation speakers throughout the history. Watch them speak and interact with the audience on YouTube and get your own ideas of how to create your personal motivational style.

Even if you feel that you are the most charismatic person of anyone you know, you should still spend some time practising your performance and speaking skills. If you have never performed in front of a large audience before, you should practise by speaking to smaller crowds first and then advance to the bigger ones.

Self-confidence is something that might eventually take you far. If you suddenly freeze and panic before your speech starts, it's not going to promise any good for you. Magnetize your audience and let your voice and words sink in to the audience's minds and hearts, so that they become your true fans. Inspire them. Create positive emotions, emotions of hope for better future inside them. If you can accomplish this in small circles, then you are half way to becoming a very, very wealthy person. A multi millionaire. Sell people value and they will bring value to you.

Your income as a public speaker depends on several different things. If you are representing you own business that provides motivational speaking services, then you can set your own prices and affect your own income. If you have a deal with another company that organizes the event, your income depends on whether the payment is fixed or commission based. The more famous and valued you get as a motivational speaker, the more valuable your services will become respectively. That's why you should always strive to enhance your brand, get a lot of positive publicity and lots of testimonials. Let this so called positive feedback loop grow your brand as much as it can. This will lead you to millions of dollars in profit.

Epilogue

I hope my book inspired you and gave you the right kind of tools to build your wealth from now on.

Go out in the world and make the best of your newly found knowledge and don't forget to inspire others!

www.ingramcontent.com/pod-product-compliance
Lightning Source LLC
Chambersburg PA
CBHW071216210326
41597CB00016B/1839

9789529352968